"If you are longing to live your life the way it is meant to be lived in Christ, you'll see how one daily devotion can energize your life in a refreshing, intimate, and challenging way. It must be read prayerfully and slowly if it is to have its full effect. Read on . . . and enjoy."

— CHUCK FLOWERS, youth evangelism consultant,
Baptist General Convention of Texas;
founder of See You at the Pole

"Mark has done an incredible job of presenting biblical truths in a very 'outside the box' format. Much of ministering to today's young people is about relevance. Mark has captured that relevance and coupled it with truth and authenticity."

— JUSTIN COFIELD, the Justin Cofield Band;
worship leader, Paradigm Bible Study, Lubbock, Texas;
worship pastor, Vista Community Church, Austin, Texas

"Whenever I read the writings of Mark Tabb, I realize two things. One, this guy is very *aware*. He soaks in life's situations. And two, he is gifted at communicating God's Word as it relates to this crazy and sometimes fascinating life. *Greater Than* is forty prime examples of Mark's ability to put God's Word and will into our everyday lives."

— CLAY CROSSE, recording artist

TH1NK
™

Go   Ahead :

TH1NK: *about God*

about life

about others

Faith isn't just an act; it's something you live—something huge and sometimes unimaginable. By getting into the real issues in your life, TH1NK books open opportunities to talk honestly about your faith, your relationship with God and others, as well as all the things life throws at you.

Don't let other people th1nk for you . . .

TH1NK for yourself.

www.th1nkbooks.com

GREATER THAN

Unconventional Thoughts
on the Infinite God

Mark A. Tabb

Th1nk Books
an imprint of NavPress®

TH1NK is an imprint of NavPress. TH1NK and the TH1NK logo are registered trademarks of NavPress. Absence of ® in connection with marks of NavPress or other parties does not indicate an absence of registration of those marks.

ISBN 1-57683-606-1

Cover design by Arvid Wallen
Creative Team: Terry Behimer, Liz Heaney, Arvid Wallen, Kathy Mosier, Laura Spray, Pat Miller

Unless otherwise identified, all Scripture quotations in this publication are taken from the *Holy Bible, New Living Translation* (NLT), copyright © 1996. Used by permission of Tyndale House Publishers, Inc., Wheaton, Illinois 60189. All rights reserved. Quotations noted as NIV are taken from the HOLY BIBLE: NEW INTERNATIONAL VERSION® (NIV®), Copyright © 1973, 1978, 1984 by International Bible Society, used by permission of Zondervan Publishing House, all rights reserved.

Tabb, Mark A.
  Greater than : unconventional thoughts on the infinite God / Mark A.
Tabb.-- 1st ed.
    p. cm.
  Includes bibliographical references.
  ISBN 1-57683-606-1
  1. God--Meditations. 2. Students--Religious life. I. Title.
  BT103.T32 2005
  231--dc22

                        2004022021

Printed in the United States of America

1 2 3 4 5 6 7 8 9 10 / 09 08 07 06 05

FOR A FREE CATALOG OF
NAVPRESS BOOKS & BIBLE STUDIES,
CALL 1-800-366-7788 (USA)
OR 1-416-499-4615 (CANADA)

Contents

Acknowledgments

A special word of thanks to my youngest daughter, Sarah, who continually asked for this book. Without you, it never would have become a reality.

Thank you as well to Terry Behimer of NavPress for catching the vision that became this book and to Liz Heaney, the best editor I've ever had the privilege of working with.

> I

Where Are You?

It was the first question God ever asked a human being. The two people who heard it fall from His lips didn't want to answer. They preferred hiding in the dirt under a bush. Both felt ashamed, but until God showed up and started asking questions, they didn't realize it. They were too busy admiring their keen fashion sense and their hot new clothes made of fig leaves. Then God's voice began echoing through the trees, and they dove for cover. I wonder, did the fig leaves hold up? Somehow I doubt it.

The next scene in the story would be funny if it weren't so tragic. Imagine it with me if you will. Adam and Eve crouch under a bush, hiding from God because they don't want Him to see them. If you listen closely you can hear them whispering, "Shhh, keep still. Maybe He won't look this way." Then Eve shifts her weight, snapping a twig under her right foot, and Adam shoots her a look. Or Adam coughs and Eve sends an elbow into his ribs, which makes him let out a muffled "Ow!" As God passes by on one side, they duckwalk around to the other, all the while hoping to escape notice.

Their situation should have struck them as odd. Hunkered down behind the bush, they should have looked at one another and asked, "Why are we hiding?" They'd never hidden before. Before this day, the sound of God moving in the garden had never struck them with fear. Now fear came instinctively. The moment they heard God, they ducked for cover; hiding from Him had become a reflex. The two had their first taste of fallen human nature.

Then God spoke. "Where are you?" He asked, but not because He didn't know the answer. The Lord of the universe, the Creator of heaven and earth, knew Adam and Eve were on the other side of the shrubbery. He didn't ask the question for His benefit but for theirs. "Where are you?" Buried beneath His words is another question: "Why aren't you here with Me?"

As we dive into this forty-day devotional, I want you to stop and listen closely. If you do, I think you will hear God asking you the same question: "Where are you? Where are you in your relationship with Me?"

You know the question is important; at least it is when you sit down with a Bible and do the whole God thing. "Yeah, I know," you tell the book in front of you, "I need to be closer to God. Just give me a Bible verse to read, an outline for a prayer to pray, and let me get on with my day. I know the routine. I've done this before."

That's always the answer to this question, isn't it? Have you ever heard someone stand up and say, "I'm as close to God as I need to be"? Neither have I. Making such a claim is like saying that you pray enough or that you tell your mother you love her enough or that you eat enough vegetables. We all have room for improvement.

Before you get one foot out the door, I want you to back up and reconsider this question. God doesn't ask how close to Him you feel today. Could He ask a more irrelevant question? How close to God do you *feel?* Our feelings have no bearing on our proximity to the One who loved us enough to give His Son for us. I had a bad headache and an allergy attack two days ago. How close do you think I felt to God while some invisible man stood on my shoulders and whacked me in the head with a hammer? Then yesterday my headache disappeared and I went to church and the band sounded great and the songs were wonderful and all the people around me lost themselves in worship. We all felt really, really close to God. But was either experience an accurate gauge of where I am in my day-to-day relationship with God? Not really.

God doesn't want to know how close you feel to Him. Instead, He asks, "Where are you?" Of course, He already knows the answer. Do you? Where are you? Don't hide behind a wall of clichés or try to shoot the question down with a barrage of excuses. That's what Adam and Eve did when they were finally found out. They pointed fingers at each other and at the snake slithering through the dust. Both made excuses and did everything they could to keep from admitting the truth they could not hide. Adam and Eve never got honest with God or with themselves. Don't copy their mistake.

Where are you?

Over the next forty days we'll be talking about some

things that will help you find the answer. The place we will begin may surprise you. We're going to start with God, not you. Why? Because your life is not about you. It is about the God who made you, the God who loves you, the God who calls you to lose yourself in Him. If that is true—and it is—our search must begin with God. So over the next couple of weeks we're going to look deep into the eyes of God to see who He is and what He is like. Only then can you discover where you truly are in your relationship with Him.

Read the third chapter of Genesis. Think about God's question to Adam and Eve. Why did He ask it? Why didn't He just lift up the bush and expose them? Why did God ask them all of the questions He asked? If He related with them like that, how do you think He relates with you?

One other note: As you walk through these forty days, keep your Bible handy. You'll need it in order to read some of the Bible passages we'll be discussing. You'll need to look them up yourself. It's a good habit to get into. You'll also need a pad of paper and a pen. Each day has questions for you to wrestle with and thoughts to reflect upon. Think about the day's reading and form your own conclusions about the concepts and questions presented. Don't just take my word for it. I also recommend that you record what God says. How much or how little you write is totally up to you. This is your time to spend with God.

Where are you?

Where do you want to be?

Where does God want you to be?

Section One

GOD

You are worthy, O Lord our God,
to receive glory and honor and power.
For you created everything,
and it is for your pleasure that they exist and were created.

—REVELATION 4:11

God made us to know Him, to love Him, and to serve Him. Shouldn't we then find out who He is? We all have ideas rattling around in our heads. The word *God* flies across the room and an image jumps into our heads. But are our ideas accurate about who God is and what He does? Do they line up with what God says about Himself? Don't you think it's time we find out? We might be surprised at what we discover.

> 2

A Comfortable Distance

I've never seen God. I've never heard His voice whispering in my ears. I've never felt the grasp of His hand around mine. He's what you might call invisible in the physical realm. At least He is to me.

I once heard about a guy who said he saw God. Or at least he saw Jesus. It happened in the bathroom while he was shaving. Jesus just showed up in the mirror and said something like, "Good morning, Mr. Dowd. How are you today?" The guy smiled and said hello to the risen Lord of the universe and kept right on shaving.

Call me a skeptic, but no one in the Bible ever stayed so calm when God appeared to him. The sight of Him scared the life out of people. There's a story in the book of Exodus in which God appeared to the entire nation of Israel at once. They didn't actually see Him, but they heard Him. God's voice boomed out like thunder as He told them,

"I am the LORD your God, who rescued you from slavery in Egypt.

"Do not worship any other gods besides me.

"Do not make idols of any kind, whether in the shape of birds or animals or fish. You must never worship or bow down to them, for I, the LORD your God, am a jealous God who will not share your affection with any other god!" (Exodus 20:2-5)

God didn't stop talking until He gave them all ten of the commandments.

How did the Israelites respond to this encounter with God? Were they as calm as the guy shaving in his bathroom? No way. In fact, the story goes on to say,

When the people heard the thunder and the loud blast of the horn, and when they saw the lightning and the smoke billowing from the mountain, they stood at a distance, trembling with fear.

And they said to Moses, "You tell us what God says, and we will listen. But don't let God speak directly to us. If he does, we will die!" (verses 18-19)

Everyone in the Bible who came close to God responded like this. The experience left them thinking they would die at any moment. Why? Rather than come face-to-face with God, most of us prefer to keep our distance from Him. We like Him being invisible, and that's usually how He stays. We can't see Him with our eyes or hear Him with our ears or experience Him physically in any way.

Because God cannot be experienced through any of the

five senses, we think we can make Him into whatever we want Him to be. We think we can make Him loving or stern or forgiving or vengeful, unlimited in His power or confined to a narrow realm we call religion, or whatever else we want Him to be at any given moment. If we say that He doesn't care whether we spend all our time lying on the beach in the warm sunshine or doing whatever makes us happy, who can argue with us? If someone tries to disagree, we pout and spout off about some kind of an experience we had with the Divine, and that ends the discussion. After all, belief in God is a very personal thing. We get to tailor a personal God to fit our own image of who and what He's supposed to be.

But what if we're wrong?

Just because thunder doesn't roar and lightning doesn't flash around us whenever we call God the Old Man Upstairs, it doesn't mean that He approves of what we are saying. Heaven's silence does not imply consent every time we drag God's name through the muck or hate someone because of the color of his skin or any of our other favorite vices. We may say God doesn't care if we spend every Sunday catching up on our sleep or sitting in our dad's boat since "I can worship God in a boat as well as I can in a church," but that doesn't mean we're right. We're not God. We don't make the rules. We don't have the final say about who He is. Only God does; at least He does if He is truly God.

That's the heart of the problem. Most of us don't want a god who is God. We don't want to encounter the majestic Creator of the universe, the One who exists independently of all that is. If we came face-to-face with this God, He might stick His nose in our business and tell us how we ought to live. We prefer telling Him how He ought to bless our lives. The god we want makes us feel good about ourselves and helps us through life's little difficulties without demanding too much in return. When this life is over, he will whisk us away to heaven where our every desire will be fulfilled.

Deep down, many of us want a god who is much less than God. There's only one problem. That kind of god is no God at all.

Don't Just Take My Word for It

Read Exodus 20. You'll find the Ten Commandments there. Usually all we hear about them is a list of stuff we are supposed to do or avoid doing. But I'd like you to go deeper. Look at the entire chapter. What does God say about who He is? Why is this such a big deal? I'll give you a hint. The people of the ancient Near East worshipped all kinds of gods, some made out of wood or stone or gold. They prayed to rivers and trees and cows. (Holy cow! Why would anyone do that?) What was God trying to get through their thick skulls? Maybe it has something to do with showing them the truth so they could know Him personally instead of wasting their time on gods who weren't divine.

When the people caught a glimpse of who God really is, it scared them. Why? Has God ever scared you?

Bottom line question: Who gets to define God? How do you think you would respond if you came face-to-face with who God really is?

> 3

Misunderstood

My dog needs to hire a public relations firm to reshape his image. His reputation isn't exactly the greatest. Imagine an eight-inch-tall, thirty-six-inch-long, furry Bobby Knight, and you'll understand how most people see my dachshund. Surly, ill-tempered, and with a bite to go with his bark, he just doesn't make a very good first impression. He didn't with the garbage man. Is it my dog's fault he thought the guy was trying to steal our garbage cans? No wonder he tried to bite him. Like every self-respecting, nervous little dog, he doesn't entirely trust the mailman. Or the UPS guy. Or anyone else who knocks on our door. He isn't mean—just protective.

And misunderstood. My dog is definitely misunderstood. He loves nothing more than jumping up on someone's lap and spending the next six to eight hours having his neck scratched. But that's the side of him no one ever sees. All people ever see is the snarling dog straining at his leash trying to take a hunk out of the leg of the nearest male between the ages of thirteen and nineteen. For some reason my dog doesn't care much for teenage boys. People think he is mean. I say he is a good judge of character.

Those who meet my dog wonder how our family puts up with him. They question the sanity of anyone who tolerates an animal that clearly despises the entire human race. My family wonders how anyone could dislike him. All the barking and snarling and snapping is just his way of protecting those he loves. What others see as unprovoked aggression and an overall bad attitude is just his way of showing how much he cares. If people could just come to know the dachshund we know, they too couldn't help but love him.

While reading through part of the Bible the other day, I realized many people have the same trouble with God. They think of Him as a narrow-minded, hard-to-please killjoy who always has a lightning bolt handy to zap anyone He sees doing wrong. Trying to make Him happy is harder than trying to keep a fourteen-year-old guy fed—and just as frustrating. After all, the list of stuff He tells us we have to do boggles the mind. Even if we could do it all (which we can't, and He knows it because He is God and God knows everything), it still wouldn't be enough. He would nitpick and find something else wrong, something else we forgot to do. After a while we would throw up our arms in disgust and wonder who needs Him.

Is that what God is really like?

Don't Just Take My Word for It

To find the answer, read Psalm 33. It's short—only twenty-two verses. It starts off by calling us to sing songs of joy to the

Lord. That's called worship. When we see God for who He truly is, it's what we will want to do. Which again makes us ask, what is God like?

This short psalm gives us the answer. Of course, it is only part of the answer. God gave us the Bible to show us who He is and what He is like. The entire Bible is about Him. It tells His story and opens our eyes to see Him in His majesty and glory. Psalm 33 talks about a few of the qualities of God we find in the rest of the Bible. So what does it say?

Read the psalm slowly. Take a pencil or pen and underline every line that talks about God's character or the way He works. Then go back and look at every sentence you underlined and ask yourself, *What does this tell me about God?* Write down your answers. For example, you might write:

Verse 4 says, "For the word of the LORD holds true, and everything he does is worthy of our trust." That tells me God is trustworthy. It also tells me that I can trust His Word and that He will do everything He says He will do.

The point of all this isn't to turn reading the Bible into an English assignment. Instead, I'm hoping you'll take a long look at the character of God. Get to know Him. See Him for who He truly is. And then? And then worship Him. Stand in awe of Him. He isn't just a character in a book or an impersonal force permeating the universe. Far from it. He is the living God, the One whose love is greater than anything you can imagine. This God, the one true God, longs to pull you into His arms and love you.

I guess God could be called narrow-minded because He requires those who run to Him to love Him more than anything else. What kind of God would demand such a thing? Perhaps a God who loves us even more.

> 4

Not for Entertainment
Purposes Only

I received an official-looking presorted mass-mailing post-card last week. It contained important information I needed to know at once. I know this because it said right at the top in bold letters, IMPORTANT INFORMATION YOU NEED TO KNOW AT ONCE! The kind people at the Personal Enrichment Society of America had a time-sensitive message—just for me—about my future. They even included a number I could call to have all my questions about love, career, and money answered. In fact, this information was so important they had arranged for me to speak person-to-person with a specially gifted master psychic so I could learn *everything*.

I am truly touched by their concern. Imagine, a specially gifted master psychic taking time out of her busy schedule to send me this mass-produced bulk mailing. She's even standing by her phone twenty-four hours a day, just waiting for me to call. And call I must, the postcard said. They want me to be helped right now! Before the end of the month! Before it's too late! Before all my plans regarding love, career, and money go up in smoke! Of course, according to the last line of the card, this time-sensitive, life-changing information from the other realm is for entertainment purposes only.

Maybe my specially gifted master psychic knows something I don't, but I'm not too concerned about love, my career, or money right now. I've been married to the love of my life for over twenty years. I changed careers a couple of years ago, and I don't want to go through that again anytime soon. As for money, the call to the number on the postcard would take some of that away. Of course, my specially gifted master psychic might have information to help me get more money. Perhaps she knows the winning Powerball numbers for tonight's lottery drawing. But if that were the case, I would think she would use the numbers herself. After all, she'd have to read a lot of palms to equal tonight's Powerball jackpot of millions of dollars.

Rather than call the number on my presorted mass-mailing postcard, I think I will respond in a manner that shows true respect for my specially gifted master psychic. While writing this, I am sending out a special message through thought waves. Here goes. Listen in, if you have the gift. *O specially gifted master psychic, you switched my name around on the time-sensitive mass-mailing postcard you sent me. Tabb is my last name, not my first.* You would think a master psychic would have known my name is Mark Tabb, not Tabb Mark. Perhaps she did. After all, life probably gets very confusing with the futures of everyone who received the presorted mass-mailing postcard dancing in her head. Trying to keep all of us straight must be quite a strain.

I'll watch my mailbox closely for her response, but I don't think she plans on writing back. That's the problem with master psychics. They're stingy with their "for entertainment purposes only" information. They always have been. Psychics have been around for thousands of years, and they've always been as accurate as they are today, which is to say, not very often and only then by chance. People still call psychic hot-lines or stop by the strange house with the giant neon palm on the roof. The future is a frightening place. Most people would rather not face it alone.

Don't Just Take My Word for It

My specially gifted master psychic may not know much about the future, but Isaiah 46:8-10 says God does. Go ahead and read it now. This isn't the only place God makes this claim. In Genesis through Revelation, He claims to see all of human history from beginning to end. He can do that because He isn't bound by time. God sees time the way a guy on the twenty-ninth floor of an office tower sees a parade—all at once rather than a little at a time. Theologians call this God's omniscience. Simply put, it means God knows everything.

But God knows even more than what the future holds. Look at verse 10 again. Notice what God says: "Everything I plan will come to pass, for I do whatever I wish." Did you catch what that means? God doesn't just know the entire history of the human race, including your life and mine from beginning to end. He is *writing* history. He plans what He wants to do, and then He does it. And because He is God, no one can stop Him.

This ability to write history hundreds, even thousands, of years beforehand means God not only knows everything and can do everything, but He is all-powerful. Read Ephesians 2:8-10. Pay particular attention to verse 10. How does God's foreknowledge and plan affect your life? If God has a plan for you, what should you do in response? How should you approach your long-term plans and dreams?

I know it is an old cliché, but it is true. You and I don't know what the future may hold, but we do know who holds the future—and that's not for entertainment purposes only.

> 5

The Woman at
the Bus Stop

I have a friend who thinks all this talk of God and Jesus is nothing but the stuff of fairy tales. He thinks the universe just happened. God didn't make it. No one made it. It made itself.

One day I listened to him go on and on until I finally asked a question of my own. "If there is no God and evolution is true, why is there so much evil in the world? How can the supposed pinnacle of the evolutionary process be so thoughtless, so cruel?" Evil acts are everywhere. Today two bombs went off in Istanbul, Turkey, killing 26 people and injuring 450. Al Qaeda claimed responsibility. Also today, a car bomb in Iraq killed 12 and injured 40. Closer to home, a rock icon was arrested for allegedly molesting a thirteen-year-old boy. A man was ordered to stand trial for murdering his pregnant wife, and the nation paused to remember the fortieth anniversary of the assassination of President John F. Kennedy. All this happened today, and today is a slow news day.

You don't have to scour the newspaper to find evidence that people are mean. Cruelty comes naturally to the human race. A kid in a high school not far from me wanted to embarrass one of his friends, so he did a little mix and match with photos on his computer to create a picture of his friend kissing a girl both he and his friend find unattractive. Then this little genius made a couple hundred copies and posted them all over the school. Funny joke, right? That is, for everyone except the girl in the photograph. This is minor compared to what goes on every day in the typical high school.

But wait a minute. Where do we get the idea that such acts are wrong or evil? If there is no God and we are all here as a result of a random accident, who is to say what is good and what is evil? In such a world, aren't moral decisions just questions of tastes and preferences? I may prefer that people refrain from shooting one another, but who is to say I am right and they are wrong? When the universe becomes nothing more than a silent accident, we have no absolutes. We are all free to do whatever we want. Every choice becomes morally neutral. That means it's as valid for me to help an old woman cross the street as it is to throw her in front of a bus; one is not more right or more wrong than the other.

When I pointed this out to my friend, he said I was crazy. No one in his right mind could live in a morally neutral world. He is right. We cannot live in the world we create when we shove God out of the picture. But that doesn't stop people from trying. People do this all the time; it's called moral relativism. People hide behind this idea when they cheat on tests or cheat on their spouses. They try to justify their actions because of the circumstances: "I only cheated on one question—and I really needed to ace that test." "The magic was gone from our marriage, so we got divorced." But if we apply this thinking to our example of the old woman standing at a crosswalk, it doesn't take long for the idea to break down because eventually somebody will come along who *will* push the old woman in front of a bus just for laughs. There must be an absolute standard of right and wrong to condemn such an act.

God Himself defines that standard. The laws and commands in the Bible aren't just things He made up one day because He had nothing better to do. They all flow out of His character. All are extensions of His holiness.

Don't Just Take My Word for It

Read Isaiah 6:1-13. Listen closely to the song the angels sang. It describes the distinguishing characteristic of God. He is holy, holy, holy. When the people God moved to write the Bible wanted to emphasize something, they repeated it. Think of it as the biblical equivalent of putting *er* on the end of a word such as *great* to make it *greater*. However, when they wanted to show that something was really, really important, they repeated it three times. That's why the angels sang, "Holy, holy, holy is the LORD Almighty!" God is holy above all else. That's what sets Him apart from us.

God's holiness does more than show us what is right and wrong. Read 1 Peter 1:13-22. In the middle of these verses God says, "You must be holy because I am holy" (verse 16).

What does the rest of this passage say about what it means to live a holy life? How different will your life be if you take this command seriously?

Other places in the Bible compare God's holiness to a light shining in the darkness. Because of sin, our world is very dark. How will you let your light shine today? If someone were trying to decide whether Christianity is true based on what they see of God in you, what would they think?

> 6

Is He Nuts?

On the inside, the Richard J. Donovan Correctional Facility looks like every other California prison built in the 1980s. With high fences, razor wire, concrete buildings, and an exercise yard complete with basketball courts and a weight lifting area, nothing about it is any more inviting than any other prison. Yet this prison faced a unique problem shortly after it opened. The guards didn't have a problem with prisoners getting out. In fact, quite the opposite. When it came time for daily prisoner counts, the staff discovered they had too many inmates rather than too few. People weren't breaking out—they were breaking in! And staying.[1]

What makes the Donovan Prison at Rock Mountain unique is its location. It sits southeast of San Diego just a couple of miles north of Mexico. The lights of the prison were like a beacon in the night to the illegal immigrants who crawled under the large, dark-colored fence that runs as far as the eye can see both east and west along the United States/Mexico border. Immigrants would put on the standard prison clothes—a blue work shirt and blue jeans—break into the prison, and intermix with the inmate population. At night they would find an empty bed and stay as long as they could. Breaking in wasn't as hard as you might think because one of the facilities, a minimum-security unit, doesn't even have a fence.

I've visited a lot of prisons and jails in five different states, but I have never found one that made me say, "Wow, I would love to live here!" Life has to be pretty bad to make prison a step up. Most people want to get out, not in. Any illegal immigrant who slips in during the night must either be desperate or crazy, or a little of both.

What, then, does that say about someone who would leave the glories of heaven to be born in a barn on earth? That's what Jesus did. He left behind the streets of gold and angels singing His praises to travel dusty streets with sheep and cattle and with people shouting insults at Him. He had to be crazy to do such a thing, yet that's a frightening thought. Jesus said, "Anyone who has seen me has seen the Father" (John 14:9). In Christ, God became flesh and dwelt among us (see John 1:14), yet His actions leave us questioning His sanity.

Consider this: Of all the places and times in which He could have lived, Jesus chose one of the worst. The smell alone would have overpowered most of us, much less the filth and disease, but Jesus immersed Himself in it. He lived His life in the same condition in which He was born—poor. He never owned a home and many times did not know where He would find His next meal, but it never seemed to bother Him. Instead of worrying about such things, He busied Himself healing the sick and preaching the good news of His Father's kingdom.

That's what got Him into trouble. His message. If He had

just stayed silent, the authorities would have left Him alone. But He wouldn't, and they didn't. Although He preached a message of God's love and forgiveness, most people didn't want to hear it. They shouted Jesus down when He told them to turn from their sins. Every day they threatened His life and drove Him from place to place. Finally they killed Him. They nailed Him to a cross like the worst of all criminals.

Of course, none of this took Him by surprise. After all, that's why He left heaven and came to earth. He came to be mocked and rejected and to die—and only an insane person would do that. Right? No one with the power Jesus possessed would volunteer for this mission. Most of us want to escape pain and suffering and hardship. Only a fool would choose to lay down His power and sovereignty as God to suffer alongside the very people who rejected Him. He had to be crazy. Or was He?

Don't Just Take My Word for It

Read Hebrews 12:1-4. As you read, pay attention to what these verses say about who Jesus is. Keep in mind that He didn't just live in heaven before He came to earth. He sat on heaven's throne. If you want to know a little more about what that was like, check out Revelation 4–5. Think about this until you get a good picture in your head of who Jesus is and the power and authority He has.

Now think about the worst place you've ever seen. If you've lived a sheltered life, you may need to stretch your imagination here. It may be a homeless shelter or a nursing home or a poor and violent neighborhood. What would it take for you to leave your home and family and move there? What do you think would run through your head during your first night there? Do you think you could ever get used to that place as long as memories of your real home danced in your head? Now multiply this by a few hundred billion, and you'll have a very small idea of what Jesus did when He came to earth. Even then, you won't have even begun to understand His death.

So what would motivate God the Father to send God the Son on such a crazy mission? "He did this for us" is our usual response, and while technically correct, it doesn't go deep enough. Why would Jesus do this for you and me? What is there about us that would make Him leave heaven's glories to endure the worst this world has to offer? Go back to Hebrews 12 and focus on verse 2. It tells us that joy motivated Christ. He endured the unthinkable "because of the joy he knew would be his afterward." What joy could possibly be found in suffering on a cross? Was He crazy, or was something more going on? You know it has to be the latter, but why? What joy did Jesus find in suffering on our behalf? And how should His joy now change our lives? You'll find part of the answer by reading further in Hebrews 12.

When it feels like living for Christ requires too much, think about what He suffered. Let Jesus' journey from heaven to earth change your perspective on the world in which God has placed you.

> 7

The Heart of the Matter

It seems strange to belong to a movement that is, in truth, quite fragile. I don't think about it very often. But now and then the thought hits me that everything to which I have devoted my life hinges on the truth of the events of one weekend. Everything. This is true not only for me but for millions of other people around the globe. If this one event is nothing more than a fraud, all of us have been duped. Ultimately, our lives will have been wasted, squandered on a lie.

If this one event is untrue, none of us has any hope. All we can look forward to is the grave. And after that? Nothing. Nothing except the frightening possibility of standing before a God we have deeply offended by painting a picture of Him that is woefully inaccurate. If this one event is a fraud, then I am a fraud. All my talk of faith and hope is just that: talk—noise hurled through the air. If Jesus did not rise from the dead, my devotion to Him is futile.

I've staked my life—and my eternity—on what happened on a small sliver of land on the other side of the globe almost two thousand years ago. Now, I know that some who claim to be Christians have backed away from the historical reality of this teaching. They try to fit into the intellectual climate of our age and say that Jesus rose again in the hearts of His disciples while His body stayed in the tomb. But according to the documents of the faith, such views are neither Christian nor biblical. True Christianity hangs on the truth that a man named Jesus was crucified on a Friday and walked out of a tomb alive the following Sunday.

But there is more to it than that. If Jesus rose from the dead, this fact affects the life of every human being. The One who died and rose again claimed to be more than the founder of a new religious movement. He boldly declared that He was sent by God the Father to save everyone who believes in Him. What does that mean for you and me? Simply put, if Jesus rose from the dead, then you and I—and everyone who has ever lived—will someday stand before Him as our judge. He will determine where we will spend eternity, and the sole criteria upon which He will base His judgment is whether we believe He lived, died, and was resurrected.

People outside the Christian faith say this sounds more than a little narrow-minded. But that doesn't mean the story of Jesus isn't true. Like I said, I've staked my life on the conviction that it is real. Those who reject Jesus stake their lives on the conviction that His story is all a lie. Some events change the course of a nation's history. Jesus claimed that He has the ability to determine the fate of all humanity, and Scripture tells us that He backed up His claim by dying on a cross and rising from the dead. All of us are staking our futures on what we believe about this single event.

Sometimes it is easy to forget that Jesus' death and resur-
rection are the centerpiece of our faith. We get caught up in
our day-to-day lives, and the strain of juggling geometry and
history and basketball and an afternoon job crowds everything else out. That doesn't mean we forget about God. Far
from it. We try to live right and to show people Christ is real
by our actions.

But from time to time we need to step back and remember
that everything we hope for in this life and the life to come,
everything we take for granted about God and His promises,
everything that we believe makes life worth living—all of it
comes down to the fact that Jesus loved us enough to die and
rise again. His sacrifice does more than cause us to cry out
for forgiveness. Read what Paul said about the Cross and the
impact it had on his life: "As for me, God forbid that I should
boast about anything except the cross of our Lord Jesus Christ.
Because of that cross, my interest in this world died long ago,
and the world's interest in me is also long dead" (Galatians
6:14). And again, "I once thought all these things were so very
important, but now I consider them worthless because of what
Christ has done. Yes, everything else is worthless when compared with the priceless gain of knowing Christ Jesus my Lord.
I have discarded everything else, counting it all as garbage, so
that I may have Christ" (Philippians 3:7-8).

After coming face-to-face with the Cross, Paul decided
that nothing else mattered. Everything else was garbage compared to what Christ had done for him. That's the power of
the Cross. It isn't just central to the Christian religion; it must
be central in your life and mine as well.

Don't Just Take My Word for It

Isaiah wrote about the Cross seven hundred years before it happened, which lets us know that Jesus' death was always God's plan to bring humanity into a right relationship with Him. The story of Jesus rising from the dead comes one chapter after His death in the four Gospels. Spend some time contemplating the Cross of Christ today. Choose one of the five accounts of the Cross and read it. You will find them in Matthew 27, Mark 15, Luke 23, John 19, and Isaiah 53.

Read about the Cross and then throughout the rest of your day reflect on it. Think about what God did for you to save you from your sin. What does that tell you about Him?

> 8

The Story of Gus

The world has two kinds of people: cat people and dog people. Cat people allow themselves to become subservient to walking allergens that think they own the world. Dog people enjoy the company of man's best friend. No one has ever called a cat "man's best friend," except maybe a cat person. Cat people spend way too much money on pet food with names like Extravagant Feast only to watch Fluffy turn up his nose to it. Even if Mr. Fluffy ate the exact same food yesterday, today he will walk away from it as if to say, "You expect me to eat *that*? Puh-lease."

Dogs don't turn up their noses to the food that dog people pour into their bowls. You can give a dog the cheapest dog food on the face of the earth, food with names like By-product of the Purina Plant, but he won't care. The sight of food in a dish makes a dog so excited that he nearly passes out with joy. At least my dog does. He runs straight from his food bowl to my lap, where he lays his head on my chest as if to say, "You are too good to me."

Yep, the world has two kinds of people: cat people and dog people. As for me and my house, we are dog people.

And we don't like cats.

My family wasn't always this way. When I was ten, I had a cat who was my best friend. Okay, I didn't have a lot of friends, but that's beside the point. I had this cat and I loved him. Then some mean person ran over him and . . . and . . . excuse me while I wipe the tears off my keyboard. I (sniff, sniff) used to not just like cats—I loved them.

Then one day years later, when my daughters were very young, someone gave my wife and me a cat. We named him Gus because we got him shortly after buying *Cinderella* on video. Perhaps that was our big mistake, naming a cat after a mouse. We should have named him Lucifer, for this feline was the Devil in a cat suit. He was ill-tempered and hated people. Whenever anyone tried to show him affection, he responded with a hiss and a quick-moving claw. Undeterred, we still loved him. We overlooked his hissing and his repeated attempts to remove all the skin from our hands with his claws.

Perhaps we'd watched too many Disney movies, but we thought little Gus could be won over with love. He couldn't. He went out of his way to make it clear that he considered us a threat. When he wasn't scratching someone, he would disappear for days or weeks at a time. Then, out of the blue he would show up on our porch and expect us to feed him. Still, we always welcomed him back.

One day Gus wandered off and didn't return. No one went looking for him. We finally decided if he didn't want us, we wouldn't press the point. By that time we'd already replaced him with a cocker spaniel. In that moment the Tabb family decided once and for all: Dogs we love, cats we don't (with apologies to the cat lovers out there).

My relationship with Gus, my former cat, reminds me of the relationship between the human race and God. Human beings have throughout history treated God in a way that makes Gus the cat look like the picture of love and affection. God created us in His image in order that we might know Him and love Him. He did this because He loves us. All of us.

The Bible says God loves us unconditionally with a love greater than our minds can comprehend. In response to such great love, we scratch and claw at God and tell Him to leave us alone. From day one—uhhh, make that day eight or nine—we human beings have run away from Him and tried to find another god more suitable to our tastes. When no other gods could be found, we made some of our own. People still have them, even in the United States. We just don't call them gods. Most of us refer to them as money or pleasure or power or fame. Our gods don't look like the idols of old, but people worship them all the same and sacrifice anything to get them.

The trouble is that these other gods don't work very well. The moment times get tough, we go running back to the Lord like a homesick alley cat. He picks us up and loves us and feeds us and nurses us back to health (homesick alley cats always come home injured from their constant fighting). We are so grateful to God that the moment we feel normal again, we run away. Large portions of the human race not only run away, but they deny that God exists in the first place. Gazing out at the wonder and glory of His creation, they thumb their noses at Him and defiantly say, "I don't see any evidence of God."

This isn't a new phenomenon. The human race has treated God like this from the beginning of time. How does God react to our scratching and complaining and running away? Read Romans 5:6-11.

When a family owns a cat or a dog that attacks their children and harms them, the family usually has the animal destroyed. Looking at the Cross of Christ, we discover we are the animal that not only harmed God's Son but killed Him. But God allowed Him to die to save us from our sin and from ourselves. Because Christ died, we can have a loving relationship with God. He shows His love for us by loving us when we are at our absolute worst.

Don't Just Take My Word for It

Read Romans 8:31-39. Spend some time contemplating the greatness of God's love for you and don't forget to write down your thoughts. As these verses say, nothing can ever separate you from that love—including you. You don't have to be perfect to keep God's love. If that were the case, you could say you earned His love. But you didn't. God doesn't love us because we are so wonderful or so cute and cuddly. He loves us because He chooses to. Nothing will ever change His mind.

> 9

Our Father in Heaven

"The LORD is like a father to his children," King David wrote in the Psalms, "tender and compassionate to those who fear him. For he understands how weak we are; he knows we are only dust."

Most people find this description of God comforting. The thought that the almighty, Sovereign Lord of the universe, the One who spoke everything into existence, cares for us like a father does his kids drives away our fears. Tender and compassionate. Loving and kind. God reaches out to us when we need Him most. The perfect Father wipes the tears from our eyes. Paul told us to cry out to Him, calling Him "Abba," the ancient Near Eastern equivalent of Daddy. What could be better?

But the idea of an all-powerful Father in heaven doesn't make everyone run to Him, especially those whose image of a father has been shaped by a less-than-perfect example. After all, Darth Vader was someone's daddy. Those who look for Father's Day cards that say, "Dear man who was there the night I was conceived," can struggle with the idea that God is their Father. They have trouble trusting Him when the only father they've ever known consistently lets them down.

So they distance themselves from God. They don't mean to do it. In fact, they want the very opposite. But they bristle at the thought of growing too close to Him.

I know.

I've been there.

I wrestle with this myself.

My dad and I have never been close, not even when I was a little kid. He worked a lot, but that wasn't the real problem. He and my mother fought all the time. They argued over anything and everything. I guess they had loved each other at some point, but those feelings were long gone by the time I was old enough to pay attention to life in my home. Affection was replaced with screaming and flying sugar bowls. My parents stayed married only because of my grandmother. She was dying of cancer. Dealing with her youngest son's divorce would have put her over the edge. The very idea of divorce was still scandalous back in those days, especially in a family that went to church on a regular basis.

But my grandmother eventually died, and my dad moved out a few months later. My sisters and I did the weekend and holiday thing at his house after he remarried. But his second marriage didn't last long, and holidays with my dad ended not long after. By the time I started college, he had moved a few hundred miles away. He called from time to time, and when he moved closer to me, I would go over to his apartment and we'd watch baseball together. Our relationship wasn't antagonistic.

We got along fine, although our conversations never got much deeper than why the Yankees fired their manager. I didn't give the relationship a lot of thought in those days. My dad was my dad. We weren't close, but we were exactly how we always had been.

Of course, if your mom and dad still live together, most of what I've said won't mean much. If your dad is your best friend, what I have to say now won't make any sense. But because you've come this far, you might as well keep reading.

Throughout my Christian life I've struggled with prayer. I know it is important, and I've done all the prayer Bible studies out there. But it's not just prayer I struggle with. At times I have trouble trusting God. I guess I wonder when He will let me down, although He never has. To be honest, sometimes I see God as distant and not just a little bit cruel. He is my Father, but at times I see Him more as the father I've lived with than the Father He is.

This is where God takes over and invades my life with a grace I cannot fully understand. My understanding of who He is and how He works may at times be tainted by my relationship with my father, but God doesn't become who I try to make Him. He told Moses at the burning bush, "I am who I am" (Exodus 3:14, NIV). That means that nothing I do or think can change who God is. He is who He always has been, and He always has been a Father who loves His children with a love we can never fully comprehend. This truth isn't just written down in a book somewhere. It is imprinted in the very character of God, which He showers upon our lives.

Don't Just Take My Word for It

This chapter started with a promise. You can read it in Psalm 103:13-14:

> The LORD is like a father to his children,
>> tender and compassionate to those who fear him.
> For he understands how weak we are;
>> he knows we are only dust.

Revelation 7:17 takes this promise a step further as it describes God wiping the tears from our eyes.

I can remember the day and hour when I first felt God's tender hand touch my cheek and wipe away my tears. It was the night my father left, never to return. Lying in the dark, listening to the fighting going on, I cried like any normal ten-year-old boy would cry. Then I felt God reach down to comfort me. He was the perfect Father at the point of my greatest disappointment with my earthly father.

Take some time to think about your own dad. How would you describe him? Has he ever disappointed you? How has your relationship with your earthly father affected your relationship with your heavenly Father? If you've grown up with a less-than-perfect example of fatherhood, your earthly dad will probably send you running in one of two directions. Either he will make you run toward God in hopes of finding the father you've always wanted. Or he will cause you to keep your distance from the Father in heaven for fear that He too will disappoint you. Which have you experienced? Don't feel weird if the answer is both. It was for me.

Now where does God fit into this equation? How does the image of the heavenly Father you carry around with you fit the picture of God you see in the Bible? Psalm 68:5 calls God a "Father to the fatherless." What do you need more than anything else from the one Father who will always love you?

One last thing. My relationship with my dad has grown over the past few years. We still have our ups and downs, but we're getting there. The results are worth the effort.

> 10

The Red Pill

There is a hunger that drives us. We don't know what it is, but we feel it our entire lives. It is always there, like a splinter in the brain,[1] driving us. The splinter keeps us from feeling completely at home on earth. It prevents us from ever being totally satisfied. No matter what we have, we still feel we've missed out, that there must be something more. The hunger hits us at the end of Christmas morning while the wrapping paper still covers the living room floor. We feel it after all the guests leave our birthday party. We taste it when we cash our first paycheck, when we buy our first car, when we get the lead in the school play, when we score the winning basket, when we experience things we dreamed about for a lifetime. No matter how big, how exciting, how pleasurable our life, the splinter remains, leaving us empty and stirring a desire for something more.

What do we want? Peace? Joy? Purpose? Love? Perhaps. But we can find peace and still have the splinter. Moments of happiness bring joy, but they don't set us free from the gnawing inside. We can find a sense of purpose by losing ourselves in a cause, but still it isn't enough. Many think the hunger is the desire for love. After all, love is all we need. At least that's what the Beatles said. But if that's the case, why do people from loving homes or in loving relationships still feel the longing inside? What more do we want?

We don't want a what. We want a who. We long for God. Considering that this is a devotional book, you saw that coming, didn't you? We all need God in our lives to be complete. Blah, blah, blah, and yawn. Tell me something I haven't heard since my parents first dragged me to Sunday school when I was a week old. I need God. You need God. All God's children need God. Hallelujah.

But that's not what I'm talking about. We don't just need God like we need to eat green vegetables and we need to spend less time in front of the computer and more time exercising. No, deep down in the inner recesses of our souls, we want Him with an appetite that can't be satisfied any other way. God planted this desire inside us when He made us in His image. Our spirit craves Him with a desire stronger than a chocolate lover's longing for a two-pound box of See's candy (and if you've never experienced See's candy, you don't know what you are missing). Blaise Pascal, a mathematician and theologian in the seventeenth century, said that every human being has a God-shaped hole in his or her heart. Yet even this falls short of the mark. Our souls ache with a desire that can only be filled by God. We don't just need something from God. We must have God Himself.

There's only one problem. Not all people realize whom they desire. If they did, they would seek Him. But they don't and they won't (see Romans 3:11).

Does this sound odd to you? The idea of the entire human race craving God? It doesn't seem to fit the world we see around us, does it?

Even if this thought strikes us as strange, it doesn't mean it isn't true. It could mean we live in a world that is out of sorts with the way it was designed, couldn't it? Sin has corrupted the entire world and especially the human mind. Yet we cannot escape the way we were made—and we were made for God. We cannot escape the longing for Him. Ecclesiastes 3:11 describes it like this: "God has made everything beautiful for its own time. He has planted eternity in the human heart, but even so, people cannot see the whole scope of God's work from beginning to end."

David put it this way:

> One thing I ask of the LORD,
>   this is what I seek:
> that I may dwell in the house of the LORD
>   all the days of my life,
> to gaze upon the beauty of the LORD
>   and to seek him in his temple. (Psalm 27:4, NIV)

David didn't want to sit in church all day every day. Instead, he longed to sit in God's presence and bask in the glow of His beauty and wonder. Jesus captured this same thought when He compared the kingdom of heaven to a pearl so spectacular that a merchant would sell everything he owns just to have it (see Matthew 13:45-46).

We've been looking at different aspects of God's character. We've seen Him as unique, holy, loving, and powerful. Yet our image of Him will always be incomplete if we leave out His beauty. Our God is beautiful, and our souls long to see Him.

Don't Just Take My Word for It

Read Psalm 63. Note the heading of the psalm. The wilderness of Judah is basically a desert. The whole region gets less than ten inches of rain per year and can go up to six months without a drop of rain. David examined the physical thirst he felt and realized it was nothing compared to his spirit's longing for God.

What about you? How does David's desire for God compare to yours? What do you long for? Do you think your longing is really a longing for God Himself?

Read through the psalm again. As you do, contemplate the wonder and majesty of the Lord. Ask God to set your spirit free with a desire that can only be satisfied by Him. Then worship Him. Once you do, you will long for more.

> 11

From the White House to the Outhouse

Only in the United States. Only in the United States can a man go from being the most powerful man on the planet to just another guy in a matter of seconds. One minute he is commander in chief of the armed forces of the world's only superpower; the next he's on a plane back to Palookaville or wherever he came from. For four, possibly eight, years someone walks beside him with a suitcase containing the launch codes for weapons capable of ending life on the planet. Then he goes back to carrying his own suitcase that contains nothing more powerful than an electric razor.

And there's nothing he can do about it. He lacks the power. So he has to leave. End of story. Once his term is up, the president has to climb into the helicopter on the White House lawn and get out of Dodge. The codes in the suitcase all change, and the generals and admirals stop taking his orders.

All human power is limited. Even dictators who rule with an iron hand cannot control anything and everything they want. Fidel Castro may control every aspect of Cuba's economy, but he can't keep people from longing for freedom so much that they will climb into leaky rafts and set sail for Florida. Josef Stalin, the Communist dictator who ruled the Soviet Union during the thirties and forties, couldn't hold on to power forever, even though he killed over twenty million people trying to do just that. In the end, the forces of nature proved stronger than his iron will. A stroke left him speechless and visions of wolves haunted him in his old age. He died with his left hand raised, trying to drive the imaginary wolves away.[1]

I think the limitations of power we live with every day keep us from fully appreciating the power of God. He doesn't have to ask permission from anyone before He acts. Nor can the forces of nature stop Him from doing what He wants. When Jesus wanted to cross the Sea of Galilee, He didn't let His lack of a boat or a raging storm stop Him. He simply strolled across the waves. When His friend Lazarus died, Jesus brought him back to life. Demons confronted Jesus while they tormented a man who lived in a cemetery. He told the thousand or so demons to get lost and drove them into a herd of pigs. Incidentally, the demon-possessed pigs charged off a cliff into the sea like lemmings.

Jesus' miracles give us a glimpse into the power of God. The One who spoke the universe into existence can do anything He decides to do. Only God has absolute power. He declares, "I do whatever I wish" (Isaiah 46:10). As Jeremiah 32:27 declares, nothing is too hard for Him. God delights in making the impossible look routine. He told a group of discouraged people: "All this may seem impossible to you . . . but do you think this is impossible for me, the LORD Almighty?" (Zechariah 8:6). That's the power of God. Nothing is impossible for Him.

The power God wields isn't just some Sunday school truth separated from reality. If you and I will begin to comprehend the greatness of God's power for us, our lives will change radically. The Bible says His power saves us (see Romans 1:16), protects us (see 1 Peter 1:5), rescues us (see 2 Timothy 4:17), keeps us from stumbling (see Jude 24), and provides for our every need (see Matthew 6:32-33). This same power of God fills us when we need Him the most, enabling us to stand firm for the Lord and speak up when words would normally stick in our throats (see Acts 6:8-15).

We often struggle with our inconsistencies as we try to walk with God. There are times we feel like losers, as though we will never be able to be a real follower of Christ. There's a big difference between those who are real and those who talk about church and God and Jesus but live like everyone else. How can you keep from falling into that trap? How can you live for Christ consistently? The answer is simple. By relying on the power of God within you.

You may not realize it, but it is God's power, not yours, that enables you to say no to temptation. He gives you the power to live a life that glorifies Him, along with the power to tell others how wonderful He is. Everything you need He provides through His power. And this power isn't like some impersonal force. The power of God comes through the Spirit of God who dwells within us as we follow Christ (see Acts 1:8).

As you draw closer to God, He draws closer to you, and His power fills you as His Spirit takes control of your life. Just contemplate this for a moment. Kings and presidents wield limited power for a limited amount of time. But the power of God that fills you and me knows no bounds, "for God is working in you, giving you the desire to obey him and the power to do what pleases him" (Philippians 2:13).

Don't Just Take My Word for It

Read Ephesians 1:19-23 and 3:20. What words does the writer, the apostle Paul, use to describe God's power? What evidence of this power have you seen in your own life? Get specific. Where have you seen God work in a way that went beyond anything you would ever dare ask or hope? Now look at the places you struggle. Where do you need to see God exercise a little of His power right now? Read back over the ways He works in our lives. What do you need God to do in your life today?

Now for the other side of the equation. Have you ever faced a situation that made you doubt God's power? Have you ever found yourself in the middle of something that made you think God couldn't do what He says He can do? Write about it. What could God have done that would have made things turn out differently? Why do you think He didn't do this? How can you reconcile God's infinite power with unanswered prayers or worst-case scenarios coming true?

> 12

God in a Box

The following is a program-length television advertisement. The views expressed are not necessarily those of this station. . . .

Announcer: Welcome to *Amazing Theological Discoveries* with Pam Perky. (A peppy theme song starts playing as canned applause welcomes Pam onto the stage.)

Pam Perky: Thank you very much. It is my pleasure tonight to introduce a man who needs no introduction. He is the author of several best sellers, including *The Rapture and Low Ceilings; God, J. Lo, and You;* and of course, *A Bowl of Beans for the Cynical Soul.* Ladies and gentlemen, please welcome to *Amazing Theological Discoveries* Mr. John Thropeil!

Audience: Yippee.

Pam: Welcome, John. It's a pleasure to have you on your . . . er, I mean, our show.

John Thropeil: Thank you, Pam. It truly is a pleasure to be with you tonight.

Pam: Now, John, what amazing theological discovery did you bring with you to our show tonight?

John: Well, Pam, I'm glad you asked. Have you ever said to yourself, "I wish God were here right now to fix this mess I'm in"?

Pam: All the time.

John: Well, Pam, wish no more. Johnco Industries is proud to announce our newest product: God in a Box. (Holds up a box.) Everything you ever needed in an almighty, eternal Lord is now reduced down to one easy-to-carry container, God in a Box.

Pam: John, I think the studio audience would agree with me that this is truly amazing!

Audience: Yeah.

Pam: Now, John, I just have to ask. How were you able to shrink thousands of years of theology down to one handy and, might I add, attractive box?

John: Well, it wasn't easy. As you know, people have been trying to shrink everything you need to know about God down to one handy container since Moses walked down off the mountain with two stone tablets in his hands. But stone tablets are hard to read and even harder to carry. So we at Johnco came up with an easy-to-use, commandment-free God, God in a Box.

Pam: That's amazing.

John: And, Pam, have you ever noticed how many words are in the typical Bible today?

Pam: I sure have.

John: But who has time to read all those words? Even if you take the time to read them, who can understand them?

Pam: I know I can't.

John: And you're not alone. So our God in a Box comes in our exclusive, doctrine-free formula. No verses to memorize, no beliefs to hold, just God, God in a Box!

Audience: Yippee.

John: There are no churches to attend, no offering plates to pass, and no sermons to doze through. With God in a Box, you don't need any of them! Why? It can all be summed up in these nine little words: God in a Box wants to make you happy!

Pam: That is truly amazing. Now let's talk to members of our studio audience who have tried God in a Box. How about you, young lady, have you tried God in a Box?

Young woman: I sure have, and I love it. See, like there was this cute boy in school that I like really liked, and he wouldn't ask me out so I like asked God in a Box about it, because going out with this boy would make me like really happy. And the next week he like asked me out.

Pam: That's amazing.

Young woman: But that's not all. After we'd gone out a few times, I like really started to like get bored with him because he like wanted to talk about something other than me. So I like dumped him. And I like felt sort of bad about it because he had just given me this like really expensive necklace and I like didn't want to give it back. But then I like remembered the nine-word secret of God in a Box, and I like knew that keeping the necklace would make me happy, so that's what I did. Like.

Pam: Audience, wouldn't you agree that this is truly amazing?

Audience: Yeah.

Me: Time to change channels. . . .

Away from television and back to reality . . .

God in a Box may not exist, yet the idea behind it is very popular. Many people believe God exists for the sole purpose of making them happy—at least that is how they behave. And if they aren't happy, God must not be doing His job. But is that true? Does God want us to be happy all the time?

Don't Just Take My Word for It

Read Psalm 34:1-10. King David, the man who wrote it, sounds pretty happy, doesn't he? Now for the rest of the story. At the beginning of the psalm are these words: "A psalm of David, regarding the time he pretended to be insane in front of Abimelech, who sent him away." You will find the story in 1 Samuel 21:10-15. David wasn't yet king; a guy named Saul was. But David was Israel's greatest hero. That is, until King Saul decided to try to kill him. David escaped, but he had no place to go. The people who once sang songs about him had turned against him. The only way he could keep from being caught by Saul was to go to one of the cities of Israel's archenemy, the Philistines. But David had fought against the Philistines and even killed their champion, Goliath. To prevent the Philistines from killing him, David pretended to be insane. He drooled down his beard and scratched at doors and acted like he was out of his mind. Does that sound like a happy time in David's life?

So here's your question of the day: Does God want you to always be happy? Why or why not? If God doesn't exist to make you happy, then why does He exist? What is the centerpiece of His plan for the universe? Check out Revelation 4:11 and Romans 11:36 for a hint. One more thing: If happiness isn't at the top of God's priority list for your life, what is?

> 13

God by Any Other Name

Some people say God has been shoved out of the public eye, but don't tell Hollywood. The Almighty has always been good for a story line or two in movies and television, and that doesn't appear to be changing as we move further into the twenty-first century. His presence lies just below the surface in the *Matrix* trilogy, directing Neo (Keanu Reeves) as he saves the human race by sacrificing himself. In *Signs*, God is the real villain, at least in the eyes of Graham Hess (Mel Gibson), even as evil aliens try to harvest human beings for food. The angels in *Touched by an Angel* do God's work for Him as they invade the lives of people to let them know God loves and cares for them. In the current television series *Joan of Arcadia*, God appears in the form of a janitor, a lunch lady, and a cute guy with a backpack, among others, as He asks a high school junior named Joan (Amber Tamblyn) to carry out His instructions.

Yet, with one or two rare exceptions, the God of the movies and television isn't the God of the Bible. The Hollywood God is far more generic and less demanding. Usually He sidesteps religious questions, even though most people have trouble thinking of God apart from religious beliefs. This God's message overflows with affirmations of His unconditional love and acceptance. He is simply God unlabeled and undefined, God the higher power at your service.

Hollywood isn't following some diabolical plot by presenting God in this way. Movie studios are out to entertain, not offend. CBS's angels who were out touching people never criticized Islam or Christianity or any other religious system because that would miss the point of the show. If its slant was against Christianity, it would also place the show at odds with many of the 80 percent of the United States population who claim to be Christians. Research has found that many people who claim to believe in God believe that all religions present different paths to the same God. George Burns in the old movie *Oh, God* summed up the feelings of many when he said, "Jesus was my son and Mohammed was my son and Buddha was my son. . . ."

I recently heard an articulate Muslim make the case that Islam and Judaism and Christianity all worship and serve the same God, albeit with different labels. Mormons make the same claim for their religion. Yet the teachings of every religion are dramatically different, as are the images of God they present. If all these paths lead to the same God, He must suffer from Multiple Personality Disorder. How else could He be the God of grace revealed in Jesus and at the same time be the gods and goddesses of Hinduism?

The Bible itself begins with one simple statement: "In the beginning God . . ." No explanations. No discussion of why

God is. Just the statement: He is God. And He doesn't sit idly, doing nothing. Genesis 1:1 tells us that "in the beginning God created the heavens and the earth." Everything that exists, from the smallest bit of quantum foam to the farthest reaches of space, came about because God spoke it into existence. On the final day of Creation, God did something different. Rather than speaking more things into existence, He scraped up some clay and formed it into a human being in His image. He then breathed the breath of life into the first man. By doing so, God made the human race completely different from everything else He made. He created us in such a way that we can know Him and love Him. That's why we exist.

From that moment forward, the central question facing the human race became: Who is God? Because God made us to know Him and worship Him and serve Him, we need to know who He is. And God isn't shy about telling us. He isn't just God, the generic higher power; He says He is the Lord God. The word *Lord* is more than a title. It is God's name, the Hebrew name *YHWH*. No one really knows how to pronounce it because the Jews wouldn't utter the Lord's name out of fear of misusing it. But they did know this: There is no god except the Lord God. He alone is God. He alone is Lord of the universe. He alone is worthy of our praise and our lives.

Read chapters 4–5 of the book of 1 Samuel. You need to read both chapters to get the full story. Israel was at war with the Philistines, and the war wasn't going well for them. In an attempt to change their luck, Israel's army decided to take the Ark of the Covenant out of the Holy of Holies in the tabernacle and carry it into battle. The Ark within the tabernacle was the place where God made His presence known in a tangible way to the Old Testament nation of Israel. When they carried it into battle, they believed God went to battle with them. In essence, this was a battle of deities. The question hanging over the battlefield was not only which nation would rule the other, but which God was real. The Israelites lost the battle, but God still prevailed. How?

The God of the Bible claims to be the only true God. All others, He says, are poor, powerless impostors. The question is not a question of religious tolerance but of truth. If the Lord is God, then we must serve Him. If Allah is God, or if Joseph Smith's exalted human being is God, then we must serve one of them. But we cannot have it both ways. The Lord God has revealed Himself for who He truly is, and He refuses to allow false gods and wrong ideas to corrupt His name.

Don't Just Take My Word for It

Earlier I said the central question hanging over the human race is: Who is God? So what is your answer? How did you come up with it? What makes your answer correct? Does there have to be a single right answer? Why?

> 14

Inquiring Minds
Want to Know

God doesn't always answer, even though the questions keep flying. If we could see Him, we would probably see a slight smile across His lips. And if we could hear Him, we'd hear silence. Nothing but silence. Some people say all the answers are in the Bible. The people who say that haven't read it, because if they had, they would know all the answers aren't there. The answers to a lot of the big questions may be there, questions such as: How can I know God and how can I be forgiven and how can I go to heaven when I die?

Those questions God answers.

But others He doesn't, questions such as: Why do bad things happen to good people and why do bad people prosper and why, if God loves everyone, doesn't everyone get to go to heaven? He never tells us how He created the universe, nor does He explain how He could make all the green plants on day three of Creation even though He didn't make the sun, moon, and stars until day four. He never clarifies why He does what He does, even though His actions don't always make sense to us. And He never answers the biggest question of all, the one we will all ask at some point in time, the question we don't so much ask as scream or cry or sigh with a whisper that can hardly be heard: Why is this happening to me?

Job asked God a lot of questions. You would too if you lived through his nightmare. In one day he lost everything he owned. His money. His flocks. His herds. His camels and donkeys. Everything people clung to three thousand years ago for wealth and security, all of it disappeared in less than twelve hours. To top it off, all ten of his children died when a storm caused the house where they were holding a party to collapse on top of them. The next day wasn't quite as bad. No one else died. Instead, Job woke up to find his body covered with boils. The sores oozed and dried in an endless cycle that left his skin black, like the color of dried blood. He fully expected to die at any moment (antibiotics and other miracle drugs wouldn't be invented for a few millennia). But Job didn't die. His body kept going forward, even though he was wracked with pain.

The reason for all of this pain seemed perfectly clear to Job's friends. They assumed Job must be a terrible sinner who was finally getting his due from God. Job knew differently. So did God. The Lord Himself pointed down from heaven at Job and said, "He is the finest man in all the earth—a man of complete integrity" (Job 1:8). But that didn't stop God from refusing to acknowledge Job's prayers. He didn't fill Job with that tingling feeling we have when we know God is near. Job was left all by himself. Everything around him screamed that God had forsaken him. In his heart he felt that it was true, and for the life of him he couldn't figure out why.

So he asked and he asked, but God never responded. When God finally did say something back to Job, He didn't answer even one of his questions. He never told His servant why his children died or why he was struck with boils or why he'd had to endure months and months of sheer agony. Nothing. Zero. Zilch. Nada. Instead, God revealed Himself in all His power and glory. He took Job on a little tour of the universe and reminded him that He had made it all. He never offered Job an explanation for the trials he had just endured, but after coming face-to-face with the Sovereign Lord, Job didn't care. He didn't need answers to keep going forward with God.

Don't Take My Word for It

All of this may not have made much sense to you. You may be thinking to yourself, *I've never had any questions for God*. If that's the case, you need to remember the wise words of Yoda to Luke Skywalker in the movie *Star Wars*: "You will, young Skywalker, you will." These words sound better with Yoda's creepy voice that sounds like Grover with a head cold. Questions inevitably arise in our relationship with God because He leaves so many gaps in our knowledge of how He works. Someone long ago said the Lord works in mysterious ways. What an understatement.

And when God does explain Himself, He usually doesn't go into as much detail as we would like. The first chapter of the Bible tells us God spoke, and voilà, instant universe. But the Bible never tells us why God made cockroaches or why ducks and platypuses and some varieties of catfish have bills for noses. Then there is you. You stand in front of a mirror and look at yourself, and you hear the Bible say you are created in God's image. Then why did He give you that nose or those eyebrows or that chin—or whatever physical feature you don't like about yourself (and we all have at least one)?

So what does God give instead of explanations? Read Job 40:1-10. What did God tell Job? Can you hear it? If not, read Job 38:1-7. Can you hear it now?

Before you read on, think this through for a moment. This question isn't just an academic exercise. Many people walk away from God because of their questions. They want answers, and God doesn't give any, so they leave. I hope you won't be one of those people. Like I said, eventually something will happen in your life that will make you question God. In that moment, His answer will probably be the same answer He gave Job. Are you ready for it? Here it is: After all the pyrotechnics, after all the displays of His power across the canvas of the universe, God told Job nothing more than this: "I am God. Not *a* god, but *the* God, the God who designed and spoke the universe into existence. Trust Me." Is that enough for you? It was for Job. God could give us a detailed explanation, but we wouldn't understand it. Remember, God is God and we are not. But also remember, He is God and He does not change. We can trust Him. The Bible says people who please God live by faith. If God gave us all the answers, we wouldn't need faith, but God knows we can't live without it. That's why the mystery remains. That's why questions go unanswered. Instead, He simply says, "I am God. Trust Me."

Will you?

Section Two

QUESTIONS

Who dares to ask [God], "What are you doing?"

—Job 9:12

Job wondered who would dare ask God about His actions, yet sometimes we want to. We wonder why God allows war and suffering and injustice to run free in our world. We get really ticked at Him, questioning whether or not He knows what He is doing. Then we catch a glimpse of the real nature of the human race, and we have to wonder how we can be the way we are. Why does God put up with us, much less love us?

Following Christ by faith doesn't mean ignoring these questions or pretending they don't exist. Instead, we need to face them head-on. We might not find the answers, but if we can see our questions in light of who God is and what He does, they will start to make a little more sense.

> 15

The Killer Inside

He's only eight inches tall. You would think a flying mammal wouldn't have to worry about him. But then again, the flying mammal didn't count on the ceiling fan knocking him to the ground and bringing him face-to-face with the eight-inch-tall dachshund. A fifty-nine-inch-tall girl walked into the room, saw the bat lying on the ground, and ran for cover. She hid in the garage along with her two sisters and mother. Not the dog. Instinct kicked in, and he jumped into action. He tracked the bat to a stack of boxes next to the basement door, jumped over the top, and ripped it out of its hiding place. Bats make a very strange sound when shaken violently by a wiener dog.

The dog became the hero of the house. All the women hugged him and kissed him and praised him for saving them from the ferocious, five-ounce bat. The bat-killing dachshund didn't sleep in his own bed for at least a week. The family let him sleep on the couch or at the foot of someone's bed, or anywhere he wanted. For a couple of days his name changed from Frank to Bruce Wayne. And forget about dog food. Bruce Wayne ate whatever he wanted. After all, that's how you treat a hero.

Now low-flying mammals will think twice before flying through our back door. The word spread throughout our small town: A vicious hunter prowls the halls of our house. A bat-catching machine. I'm even thinking about renting him to the Methodist church down the street. They have a major bat problem. Let me put it this way: You don't want to crawl through their attic anytime soon. I think they would pay any price for the services of the dachshund who fears no bat, big or small. One day in that attic, and the Methodist bat problem would be gone. Forever.

The strange thing is, I never trained my dog in the fine art of bat hunting. I didn't tie a toy bat on a string and let Frank practice leaping into the air at just the precise moment. Bat catching wasn't even an elective at obedience school. All this time I thought he posed a threat only to dog food and stray socks lying on the living room floor. I never dreamed that inside my hyper little dog lurked the heart of a killer—a natural-born bat killer.

I wonder what other dark secrets lurk in the inner recesses of my dog's soul. I think his docile lapdog act is just a front. There's more to him than the creature that spends 60 percent of the day sleeping and 40 percent barking at himself. He is by instinct a hunter. A short hunter, but a hunter nonetheless. When the opportunity presents itself, that instinct takes over. He doesn't have to stop and think about what he is doing. Catching a bat in midair and shaking it until it doesn't ever want to fly again comes naturally to him.

I hate to admit it, but I enjoyed watching the dog shake the bat. My heart was pounding during the hunt, and when

Frank grabbed the bat and threw his head from side to side as fast as he could while the bat's leathery wings slapped him on the nose, a smile broke out across my face. I too wanted the bat to suffer and die for invading my happy home and upsetting my family. I wanted him to endure the pain of all the bats who've flown through my house over the years. Whether the bat is now in bat hell, I will not say because members of PETA may pick up this book. Suffice it to say, he won't be coming back to the green house on Washington Street anytime soon, if you catch my drift. You couldn't hear it, but an evil laugh erupted in the room as I penned that last sentence. There's a bit of a bat killer in me as well.

And there probably is in you. You may not know it, but just let one of those disgusting creatures do a few loop-de-loops in your living room, and watch out. A flood of emotions will explode to the surface. Animal lover? Hah! You may find all wild creatures to be cute and adorable, but that will change the moment your house becomes a bat sanctuary. You'll wish you had a dachshund trained in the fine art of bat defense. These thoughts may horrify you, and you may suppress them as quickly as you can, but a dark side lingers within your soul. All it will take to bring it to the surface is one small bat flying next to the ceiling fan or a rat scampering across your dining room floor.

What other dark secrets lie inside our souls, waiting to assert themselves when the opportunity presents itself? God knows the dark secrets that lie inside of you and me. He told the prophet Jeremiah, "The human heart is most deceitful and desperately wicked. Who really knows how bad it is? But I know! I, the LORD, search all hearts and examine secret motives. I give all people their due rewards, according to what their actions deserve" (Jeremiah 17:9-10). God can see everything inside of us—every secret desire, every unseen motive. He doesn't just glance occasionally to see what is there. He searches our hearts and carefully examines our secret motives. Nothing is hidden from Him. Nothing is secret to Him. Who we really are lies before Him like an open book.

Don't Just Take My Word for It

Who we really are creates one of the biggest obstacles we will ever face. When bad things happen, we throw questions at God, asking Him why He would allow them to take place, yet when we look deep inside ourselves, we find the answer. Read Romans 7:14-25. These verses describe the battle that rages inside us between who we are in Christ and our old, sinful nature.

When do you feel this battle raging? It takes different forms in different situations. For example, on dates a fight breaks out inside you between the desires of your hormones and the commitment you made to God to remain sexually pure. On the job it is a fight between doing just enough to get by and the Scripture ringing in your head telling you to do your work as for the Lord (see Colossians 3:23). What situations cause the fight to reach new levels? Get specific. And get honest. In the heat of the battle, which side do you want to win? Go back to Romans 7:14-25. What help do you have in the midst of these battles? How does this help work? What is your part of the equation? Check out 1 Corinthians 10:13 for help with the last question.

> 16

Bad Guys Finish First

Idi Amin died in his sleep on August 16, 2003, in his home in Saudi Arabia. He had fallen into a coma a few days earlier, a coma from which he never awakened. Witnesses described the scene as very peaceful. Amin's four wives gathered around him as he slipped from this world into the next. He was eighty. The former Ugandan dictator's family wished that the man who called himself Big Daddy could have gone back to his beloved homeland to die, but the current Ugandan government refused their request.

Instead, Idi Amin died in his adopted homeland, the place where he'd lived for over a decade. The Saudi government welcomed him after he moved there from Libya, where he'd lived since he was driven from power in Uganda in 1979. In some ways he lived like any other retiree. He had saved for retirement by stealing money from Uganda and decimating its economy. Once his money ran out, the Saudis stepped forward and gave him a regular monthly stipend. In his last interview, given in 1999, the former despot reported that he lived a quiet life. He thought most people in Uganda no longer held a grudge for the hardships he had inflicted upon them.

Perhaps he was right. After all, who couldn't forgive his small excesses. During his eight years in power, he killed or caused the disappearance of only three hundred thousand to five hundred thousand people. The records are a little sketchy because anyone who criticized Amin's regime quickly disappeared himself. He dissolved the police force when the officers who tried to investigate his crimes ended up dead. Amin wielded one of the most powerful weapons of mass destruction ever devised by man: angry mobs of followers. Hitler caused the trains in Germany to run on time; Amin did the same thing with death squads. At the same time every day, he would gather his critics into one place and have his goons bludgeon them with sledgehammers. Because he would never ask anyone to do something he wouldn't do himself, Amin often joined in the killing personally.

Being an enemy of Idi Amin might have been risky business, but being a friend or family member didn't guarantee safety either. He beat one wife to death and then dismembered her body. Big Daddy also killed one of his sons and, upon the advice of a witch doctor, consumed his heart. This ritual cannibalism was supposed to give him even greater power.

The world knew of Amin's crimes against the Ugandan people but did nothing to stop him. In fact, they did something worse than nothing. They spurred him on. Amin received a standing ovation from the General Assembly of the United Nations in 1975 when he delivered a speech calling for genocide against the nation of Israel. His remarks brought down the house. Amin also supported international terrorism, employing Soviet-trained Palestinian terrorists as his own personal bodyguards.

Idi Amin disappeared from the public eye when he was driven from power by the Tanzanian army in 1979. His old friend Muammar Gadafy, the Libyan dictator, offered him exile and welcomed him into his country. The crimes Amin committed and the five hundred thousand or so people who disappeared during his reign faded from public memory along with the crazy old dictator who once declared himself the king of Scotland and the conqueror of the British Empire. No international tribunal ever sat and passed judgment upon him. Nor did his face ever appear on a deck of playing cards produced by the Pentagon to help identify war criminals. Instead, Idi Amin settled into retirement with his four wives and the millions he had stolen from his former homeland.[1]

The picture of Idi Amin dying peacefully in the finest hospital in Saudi Arabia is the very definition of injustice. One has to wonder if the world would have stayed so quiet if his victims had been European rather than African or if Uganda was a major oil-producing nation. But the world shrugged, and Idi Amin Dada became little more than a footnote to the history of the 1970s. Watching him escape the consequences of the genocide he unleashed is enough to make an atheist hope Amin will receive some sort of eternal retribution beyond the grave.

Where was God while Idi Amin butchered thousands of helpless people? Even if Amin wasn't brought to justice by the nations of the world, couldn't God at least have made him die a horrible death? After all, look at what happened to King Herod: "Immediately, because Herod did not give praise to God, an angel of the Lord struck him down, and he was eaten by worms and died" (Acts 12:23, NIV). Wouldn't the same sort of death make a much better ending for this story?

We soon learn while living on planet Earth that justice doesn't always prevail. Bad guys don't always get theirs in the end, and good guys don't always live happily ever after. Read Hebrews 11:35-40. There you will encounter the stories of people who loved God yet died before their time. They suffered and were hunted down, yet they refused to deny God. How can we reconcile the picture of godly saints being sawed in half with that of a brutal dictator dying in his sleep while his four wives looked on? Does this mean God is unfair?

If this world were the end of the story, the answer to the last question would be yes. God would be unfair. But the story doesn't end when time comes to a close.

Don't Just Take My Word for It

Read Revelation 11:15-18. How does the Bible say God will set things right at the end of time?

Justice will prevail on the day Jesus returns to judge the earth. But between now and then, He calls us to do something. He calls us to stand up for the oppressed and to work for justice. Read Amos 5:21-24. God is far less impressed with all our religious words than He is with seeing our words translated into action on behalf of those who can't stand up for themselves.

Look around your world. Look at your school, your neighborhood, your community. Do you see anyone who is being treated unfairly? Do you see anyone who is oppressed and can't do anything about it? How can you be part of a "flood of justice" while also sharing God's grace with those who hurt? Injustice doesn't just happen on the other side of the globe. Now what will you do?

A Better Plan

The other day I was watching *The Andy Griffith Show* and a commercial came on for a truck-driving school. Because I have no interest in becoming a truck driver, I did what I do every time a commercial comes on: I grabbed the remote and started cruising through the channels. Since our home is the only home in the country without cable *or* satellite (I know, we live in the dark ages), it didn't take long to make the full loop and come back to the *Andy Griffith* station. But Andy still wasn't back. Some attorney was on the screen, telling me he will fight for me to keep me from getting stuck with a tiny little check from the insurance company, and as I haven't been hurt in an accident lately, I went back to channel surfing.

Then, for no apparent reason, I paused on a local Christian station where three or four people all dressed in coats and ties and Sunday dresses were talking about how to reach Iraq for Christ. I want to see Iraq reached for Christ, so I put down the remote and listened.

Here was their ingenious plan for reaching the Islamic population of Iraq: satellite television. They planned to launch another satellite that would begin beaming television signals toward the Persian Gulf. Because most people lack the ability to pull satellite television transmission waves out of the air telepathically, the people wearing coats and ties and Sunday dresses asked the audience to pray. They asked me to pray that the people in Iraq would get good enough jobs to be able to afford to buy a television. And a satellite dish. And monthly satellite television service. And they asked me to pray that after they bought all these things, the good people of Iraq would then happen upon this Christian television program while channel surfing during commercials of *Andy Griffith* reruns. They also wanted me to pray that the people of Iraq would then pause long enough to hear the gospel and believe in Christ as their personal Savior.

Amazingly, the people on the program didn't see the absurdity of this idea. There has to be a simpler way for the people of Iraq to hear about Jesus. Here's what I came up with: I think God should write the gospel in the sky. One clear day, and most days in the desert are clear unless there happens to be a sandstorm, a giant hand should appear in the sky and start writing the gospel in Arabic. Then all the people in Iraq could look up at the sky and read the gospel and believe. What could be simpler? In fact, I think God should do this in every nation in the world. Everyone would fall to their knees and confess Jesus as Lord if they could see His hand with their own eyes, writing His message across the sky.

I know what you're thinking. You think I've lost my mind coming up with such a crazy plan. To that I say, O *contraire!* God once used a variation of my plan. A giant hand didn't appear in the sky, but it did appear in a room. Daniel 5 tells of the time a hand appeared and started writing in the plaster on a wall during a party the king of Babylon threw for himself. Read it for yourself. Everyone in the room freaked out and started screaming, and the king turned white as a ghost. It wasn't just the hand that scared them. The words the hand of God scrawled in the plaster got their attention as well. If this plan worked so well 2,500 years ago in a single room, why wouldn't it work even better today in the skies over Iraq?

I think it would. After all, who could deny the existence of God after watching His hand write in the sky? Who could dispute the facts of the gospel after reading them in the clouds? Everyone would see and believe. They would have to. Why doesn't God try it?

That's the real mystery. Why doesn't God make Himself known by writing in the sky or by performing some other big, spectacular miracle? After all, seeing is believing, and if the people of the world could just see some tangible evidence for the existence of God and the truth of the gospel, they would have to turn to Christ. Wouldn't they?

Don't Just Take My Word for It
Read Psalm 19:1-4 and Romans 1:18-20. The beauty and glory of creation already tell the world that God exists. All people have to do is look up at a clear night sky and they will realize a glorious God made all of this.

But is that enough? Go back and reread Romans 1:18-20. Does nature tell people enough about God for them to believe in Jesus and be saved? It's an easy question, and the right answer is *not* yes.

That's why God wrote the truth of the gospel in two other places. The first is the Bible. The second is you. Read Matthew 5:13-16 and 1 Peter 2:11-12. Your life is the tablet upon which God has written His message. If you live your life for Christ, those around you can't help but come face-to-face with the living God. Or, if you act just like everyone else, they may decide the whole Christianity thing is a fraud. Your life proclaims a message. How you live determines what that message will be.

God reveals Himself to the world through believers like you and me. Because that is true, how do we need to live our lives? Remember, just being good and moral doesn't cut it. I know moral atheists. How should you live so that people will see Christ in you?

You and I have a responsibility that stretches around the world to the millions of people who have never heard of Jesus. Since they can't afford satellite television, how else can they hear the gospel? Perhaps someone needs to go to them. How can you be a part of the process? You can't go everywhere in the world by yourself. How can you help the people who go around the world personally telling people about Jesus? What can you do to support them? Will you?

> 18

What If They Refuse?

Jim walked into his freshman classes with an announcement for his teachers. He said that although he had to attend class, he didn't intend to learn anything. Failing grades and all the parent-teacher conferences in the world wouldn't change his mind. Jim made it clear that he didn't care for school. Occupying a desk was all he planned to do for the next nine months, and he would defy anyone who tried to make him do more.

A quarter of the way through the school year, that's exactly what Jim has done. He's earned a D or an F in every class, including those he must eventually pass if he plans to graduate from high school. But that's the beauty of Jim's plan, at least in his eyes. He doesn't plan to graduate. At some point in the next year or two, he will stop attending school altogether. His days will then consist of sleeping late and trying to break his latest high score on PlayStation.

Before that day arrives, he will fill in random circles on the standardized test answer sheets, bringing down the overall average for the entire school. Next year, when he fails the graduation exam every sophomore in his state must take, he'll become one of the statistics politicians from state capitals and Washington, D.C., love to throw around. By that point, no one will know about the efforts of one teacher after another to get Jim to care. Nor will they know about the announcement Jim made in his freshman classes. Instead, Jim the Statistic will be Jim the Child the System Failed and one more reason why the education system in the United States must be reformed.

Yet the vast majority of education reform movements ignore one minor fact of life: No one can force Jim to learn when he refuses to be educated. While he can be forced to sit in a desk and hear a teacher talk about the War of 1812 or how $a^2 + b^2 = c^2$, no one can make him process the information hitting his ears. Men in blue suits with red ties earn loud applause when they talk about holding teachers accountable, yet how can we hold them responsible for the failures of a child whose only goal was to fail? That's like holding the chef responsible for the bulimic coughing up her dinner in the restaurant bathroom.

Jim's teachers aren't being unfair when they refuse to pass him along to the tenth grade. In fact, they are being the exact opposite. Giving Jim the grades he deserves is the very definition of fairness. You might even call it an act of generosity, giving him the failing grades he wanted so much that he was willing to ignore every homework assignment and not study for a single test. A great deal of effort goes into failing so miserably. The slightest effort might have earned him a C, so he had to be careful to do even less.

In the same way, people call God unfair when they read in His Word that those who do not believe in Jesus Christ will be separated from God forever. "How could a loving God send anyone to hell?" they protest. Maybe they have a point. After all, hell is a horrible place. The Bible describes it as a place where the worm never dies and the fire is not quenched (see Mark 9:48). *Worm* refers to garbage-eating maggots. In hell, people will be tormented forever, as if they had been cast into an eternal garbage dump. Matthew 25:30 also calls hell a place of outer darkness, filled with weeping and gnashing of teeth. How could a loving God send anyone to such a place?

But the worst part of hell isn't the fire or the worms or the darkness. Hell is hell because it is a place where creatures created to know God are separated from Him forever. God made us in His image in order that we might love Him and have an intimate relationship with Him. That's our purpose. That is why we were made.

Yet most people on earth don't want anything to do with God. Read Romans 3:10-18. These verses describe the sin of the human race. Our entire species turned away from God. Sin is far more than drinking or cursing or sleeping around. The heart of sin is telling God to leave us alone or reducing Him to a handy, easy-to-use good luck charm, devoid of power. Either way, we make it clear to the Almighty that we plan to live our lives our way, and He is cordially invited to leave us alone.

People don't have to know about Jesus to do this. Romans 1:18-20 tells us that God reveals enough of Himself through nature for people to know He exists. He also gave us His Word so we might know Him, and He sent His Spirit to draw the world to Himself (see John 16:5-15). But most people ignore Him. Instead, they worship false gods or even themselves. Other people set out to prove themselves good enough to be let into heaven on their own. They want to show that they don't need God to change their lives, thank you very much. More than anything, they miss the point of why they exist—to know God. They respond by telling Him to get lost.

So is God unfair when He separates sinful people from Him forever? No. Just the opposite. His actions show justice being carried out. Fair and just means giving people what they deserve.

Don't Just Take My Word for It

Read Ezekiel 18:23-29. How does the passage describe God's fairness and justice? What does God do with people who refuse to believe in Him or obey His Word? Before you read on, please answer this question: What do you think God should do with those who will not turn to Him? C. S. Lewis answered the question this way:

> In the long run the answer to all those who object to the doctrine of hell is itself a question, "What are they asking God to do?" To wipe out their past sins and, at all costs, to give them a fresh start, smoothing every difficulty and offering every miraculous help? But He had done so, on Calvary. To forgive them? They will not be forgiven. To leave them alone? Alas, I am afraid that is what He does.[1]

What do you think? Should God force Himself on those who want Him to leave them alone? Write down your thoughts. This isn't an easy question or an easy topic. Even though we can't see it now, eternity is real, more real than the temporary world in which we live today. The stakes are much higher than trying to make it through life without a high school education.

> 19

Blessing or Curse?

"Give us today our daily bread," Jesus taught His disciples to pray in Matthew 6:11 (NIV). Today, for the first time in history, this prayer is being answered. After painstaking field research (consisting of a trip to the Wal-Mart Supercenter), I can proclaim to you that there are enough varieties of bread for you to experience the ultimate daily bread. You could have a different variety every day for at least one year, maybe two. Yes, this is the age of the bread of the day. What a glorious time to be alive.

Two thousand years ago, when Jesus first uttered these words, there were two, maybe three, kinds of bread. People had to make their own. They took some wheat, ground it into flour, and baked it into bread. Depending on their tastes and the time of year, they could have their bread either leavened or unleavened, that is, made with yeast or made without. Out in the sticks, the less cultured folk—those people too poor to buy wheat—made bread out of barley. It didn't quite have the texture or the taste of bread made from wheat, but it beat no bread at all. I suppose they could have made their barley bread with yeast or without, but that was it. No variety. No "Would you like white or harvest wheat or Italian or bread topped with cheddar and Asiago cheese or Parmesan oregano bread?" accompanying every order at the local Subway. You either chose wheat or barley, leavened or unleavened, or you went without. With time, someone figured out how to turn rye and maybe another grain or two into flour, but the dark days of bread continued.

Until now.

According to the bread aisle at the Wal-Mart Supercenter, this is the Golden Age of Bread. Within the narrow category of sandwich bread alone, I found approximately 892 varieties, give or take a few hundred. Of course, there were your basic white bread and your basic wheat bread. Your butter-topped white bread and butter-topped wheat bread. Potato bread. Whole-grain bread. Five-grain bread. Seven-grain bread. Nine-grain bread. And Indian-grain bread. There were wheatberry and oatbran and Roman meal breads, breads with nuts baked in and breads with oatmeal on the crust, small breads sliced nearly as thin as a cracker and thick-sliced bread perfect for toast. There were low-fat and no-fat and bread designed to lower your cholesterol levels. As far as the eye could see, there were breads and breads and more breads spread across an aisle nearly the length of a football field. At least it felt like it was the length of a football field.

These were only the sandwich breads.

The Supercenter also had French bread and Italian bread and rye bread and pumpernickel and sourdough and dinner rolls and bread sticks and bread sticks with butter and garlic and Italian bread with herbs and garlic and garlic and herbs and butter and herbs and herbs and herbs scattered everywhere from the freezer case to the bakery. There were breakfast breads with raisins and cinnamon all swirled together in the shape of a pinwheel in each slice.

I also found bagels. Bagels in the bread aisle and bagels in the freezer near the pizzas and bagels in the refrigerator case a couple of stalls away from the butter. The bagels came in plain or wheat or honey wheat. Baked inside were blueberries or strawberries or onions or garlic or a combination of all of the above. Well, maybe not *all* of the above. A few aisles over I found unleavened bread in a box called Matzo, which looked a lot like a cracker but didn't taste quite as good as a saltine.

And if you want to wash your bread down with a refreshing glass of Pepsi, life only gets better. Back in a far corner of my local Supercenter I found Pepsi and Diet Pepsi and Pepsi One and Wild Cherry Pepsi and Pepsi Vanilla and Diet Pepsi Vanilla and Pepsi Twist with lemon and Diet Pepsi Twist with lemon and caffeine-free Pepsi, but I didn't see any caffeine-free Pepsi with lemon. Maybe next week.

What's that you say? You prefer Coke to Pepsi? Even better. There's Coke Classic and Diet Coke and of course, you can get both with a hint of lemon. You can select from Cherry Coke and Vanilla Coke and Diet Cherry Coke and Diet Vanilla Coke. Coke also makes Sprite, which comes in regular and diet and, for the really adventurous types, you can have Sprite with caffeine. And that's just the start. The average Wal-Mart Supercenter has even more varieties of soda than it has bread.

"Give us today our daily bread." Our prayer has been answered. Most of us don't even have to ask. We have bread—lots of bread. Yet somehow we still find it necessary to ask for more. Read Jesus' prayer in Matthew 6:9-13. Jesus wants us to depend on the Father for everything we need, every single day. The concept of having to pray for food each day is lost on many (but not all) of us who grew up in this country. We throw out more food than most people in the world have to eat.

Don't Just Take My Word for It

What do you think? Is our abundance of bread and other food a blessing or a curse? Before you answer, think about this: In the Bible, the better off people were, the less they thought about God and the more likely they were to stray from Him. Jesus said, "It is easier for a camel to go through the eye of a needle than for a rich person to enter the Kingdom of God!" (Mark 10:25).

Even people in the Bible who knew the Lord had trouble staying faithful when they had a lot of stuff. Don't believe me? Check out 1 Kings 10:14-29. There you will find a description of the vast wealth of the richest (and wisest) man who ever lived. Now read 1 Kings 11. What happened to Solomon's relationship with God after he grew rich and powerful?

If you didn't know where your next meal was coming from, how intense would your prayer life be right now? How intense do you want your prayer life to be?

Read about the time Satan tempted Jesus (see Matthew 4:1-11). Look closely at what Jesus said in verse 4: "People need more than bread for their life; they must feed on every word of God." What do you think this means? Do you agree or disagree with Jesus' words? Why? What evidence do you see of your answer? How different would your answer be if you didn't have any bread for today and didn't know where you could find it?

> 20

In Food Pyramids We Trust

A study conducted in 2001 found that 61 percent of Americans are either overweight or obese.[1] Sixty-one percent! Obviously, the United States government cannot allow an epidemic of these proportions to spread without doing something to stop it, and now at last they have. Our national obesity problem has finally been solved. After two years of intensive research, federal officials announced recently that they plan to reshape the food pyramid, which will lead all of us to eat better and in turn will stop our waistlines from expanding.

Apparently the reason we eat too many bad foods is because the old food pyramid used a one-size-fits-all approach. In case you haven't looked at a bread wrapper lately (which is one of the few places you can see it), the food pyramid tells us which foods we should avoid and which we can indulge in whenever we like. The bread, cereal, rice, and pasta food group rests on the bottom of the pyramid, which means we can eat six to eleven servings of food in this group per day. Above this are the vegetable and fruit groups and in the section above those, the milk and meat groups. The fats, oils, and sweets food group sits at the top of the pyramid with the words USE SPARINGLY in all capital letters. If bread wrappers could be wired for electricity, I'm sure these words would flash in red like the lights over a dangerous intersection.

The government launched the old food pyramid in 1992 to help Americans wean themselves from food loaded down with fats and to steer us toward more breads, cereals, rice, and pasta. Years later, we decided the pyramid had failed miserably and must be replaced by a newer, better, high-tech pyramid. The government hasn't yet unveiled the new key to healthy living. After all, they've only been working on it for two years. They need at least two years and probably a few million dollars more to complete the task. But once the new food pyramid is in place, we will have a "good start in solving the obesity epidemic," according to the executive director of the U. S. Department of Agriculture's Center for Nutrition Policy and Promotion.[2]

I, for one, feel much better. I'm glad the people who solved the problems of underage drinking and smoking and teen pregnancy will now lick the obesity epidemic. After winning the war on drugs by completely eliminating demand with the twin weapons of "Just Say No" and DARE, they can now help us say no to Twinkies and DARE to stay off Oreos. Just think, all we have to do to drop that sixth or seventh Krispy Kreme of the day is stop, log on to the official U. S. Department of Agriculture's Center for Nutrition Policy and Promotion website, navigate to the high-tech food pyramid page, and read these words: "Eat fat-laden doughnuts sparingly." If that won't keep us from overeating, what will?

You and I already know the answer. We eat the wrong kind of food because we want to. At least I do. Even if the president of the United States called my house and told me that eating too many Doritos will make my pants too small, I wouldn't switch to no-fat rice cakes. I like Doritos. I don't like rice cakes. And that's the real problem. It has nothing to do with information and everything to do with desire.

The people who feel obligated to tell us what is good for us have already educated us about the perils of high-fat food, just as they've told us that smoking can kill us and drugs are bad. Yet I've seen cardiologists smoking, and drug use continues to climb even though every fifth grader in the country has to go through an anti-drug education program. As long as we human beings find joy and pleasure in doing things that are bad for us, we will keep making bad choices. No food pyramid can change this fact, regardless of how high-tech it might be.

Don't Just Take My Word for It

Read Genesis 3:1-7. What role did appetite play in the first sin in human history? The serpent's temptation of Eve shows how all temptation works. It plays on natural desires that we already have by warping them and moving them beyond what is normal or healthy. But sin doesn't stop there. It lifts up our natural appetites and desires and tries to put them in God's place. That's why Paul said of people who oppose Christ, "Their god is their appetite, they brag about shameful things, and all they think about is this life here on earth" (Philippians 3:19).

This isn't the end of the story. It isn't as though our appetites alone make us do wrong, as if they grab us and force us to do things against our will. We do wrong because we want to. Go back again to Genesis 3. Notice that the snake didn't hold a gun to Eve's head. Think about your own life. How often have you been forced into sin? How often do you do wrong because you really want to, even when you know the possible consequences?

Paul described the human condition in Romans 3:9-12 and 3:23. Why are we like this? Why can't we change? Our real problem isn't a lack of information. Knowing something is bad for us isn't enough. What more will it take for genuine change to take place in the human heart?

> 21

Man on the Moon

China plans to send a man to the moon, but the news hardly caused a stir in the rest of the world. Most people yawned and said, "Hasn't that already been done?" On July 20, 1969, Neil Armstrong and Buzz Aldrin went for a stroll across the lunar surface less than a decade after President John Kennedy announced the ambitious goal. It was heralded as the greatest accomplishment in human history, and most people assumed it would be the first step toward even greater achievements.

The father of American rocketry, Wernher von Braun, predicted back in 1969, "By the year 2000 we will undoubtedly have a sizable operation on the moon, we will have achieved a manned Mars landing and it's entirely possible we will have flown men to the outer planets."[1] Few people would have argued with him. We all thought trips to the moon would become routine. Pan American Airways received more than ninety thousand applications from people who wanted reservations for the first commercial flight to the lunar surface, including one from future president Ronald Reagan.

Von Braun never dreamed manned exploration of the

solar system would come to a halt a little over three years later. Humanity's sizable operation on the moon now consists of nothing more than footprints, a couple of lunar rovers, and six American flags. Sending men to Mars still generates interest in sci-fi movies, but the closest NASA has come to the Red Planet are twin robotic rovers named Spirit and Opportunity that scooted across the planet's surface looking for water. Pan American Airways never made a commercial flight to the moon, nor will it. The pioneer in commercial aviation went out of business in 1991. Its name was revived a few years later by a regional airline in the Northeast.

The fact that the dreams and predictions generated by man landing on the moon didn't come to pass doesn't mean the lunar missions were failures. The continuing study of moon rocks has dramatically expanded our understanding of the nature of the moon. As every kid who grew up in the sixties knows, without the Apollo missions we wouldn't have Tang, the only orange drink to travel into space. Space exploration also gave us Velcro and personal computers. These two inventions alone made the whole journey worthwhile. After all, can you imagine life without Velcro or your PC?

Yet it strikes me as odd that the greatest technological achievement in the history of the human race has largely been forgotten. We don't celebrate the day as the crowning moment of science. No one throws parties, and towns don't hold parades on July 20. Neil and Buzz's fantastic journey has been relegated to the Today in History column tucked away on the back of the entertainment section of the Sunday paper. Throughout history, people looked longingly at the moon and wondered if we would ever be able to go there. Few people outside of the burgeoning Chinese space program ever think about going back.

The human race always thought that if we could put a man on the moon, we could surmount any problem. Any nation that could escape the earth's gravity could surely solve hunger and poverty. If we could put a man on the moon, we assumed that we would also be able to bring about world peace or find a clean, efficient energy source that wouldn't destroy the environment. Our dream of a manned mission to the moon came true, yet all of the problems that have plagued the human race since the dawn of time have stayed with us. We found it easier for two men to survive on the surface of the moon than for the human race to get along on earth.

Isn't it ironic? We traveled 240,000 miles into space only to come face-to-face with our limitations. We went to the moon and learned that all our determination, ingenuity, and technology cannot make life on earth the paradise we long for. We didn't find answers on the surface of the moon, only more questions. Why can't all the best minds on earth solve the problems that have been with us since the beginning of time? Why can't we solve the problem of war and bring about world peace? Why can't we get rid of drugs in schools and keep drunk drivers off the streets once and for all? Why can't we end racism and sexism and all the other "isms" that cause people to hate and harm one another?

The twentieth century not only saw men walk on the moon, but it also witnessed one unbelievable scientific breakthrough after another. Think of this for a moment: The first fixed-wing aircraft, a kite mounted on a stick, was invented one hundred years before the Wright brothers' first flight. A century went by before the kite advanced to a manned glider, yet it took less than seven decades to go from a glider to a manned landing on the moon.

But in spite of these incredible scientific advances, the twentieth century was the bloodiest century in human history with two world wars and the unleashing of nuclear weapons. In addition, millions died in the Nazi holocaust, and millions more died at the hand of Communist dictators in the Soviet Union, China, and Cambodia. What is wrong with this picture?

Don't Just Take My Word for It

Before you move on, try to answer these questions: Why can't the human race solve the problems we face every day? What keeps us from living in peace and harmony with one another and with our environment? What stands between us and our ability to create heaven on earth?

Read Romans 5:12-17. What is the source of all of humanity's problems? Now read Isaiah 55:6-9. What is the solution? Can it really be this simple? Read Revelation 19:11-21. Why would all the armies of the earth fight against Jesus? When will the problems of the earth finally be solved? Write out your thoughts.

For thousands and thousands of years people have argued with God and said our problems can't be reduced to something as simple as sin. Yet the problems persist, and all of the human race's answers have been discredited. Despite all our technological advances and discoveries, we have not yet solved the problem of sin. Do you think we ever will?

> 22

God Bless This Bomb

Early on the morning of August 6, 1945, Chaplain William Downey gathered with the flight crews of the 509th Composite Group of the 315th Bombardment Wing of the Second Air Force on Tinian Island. As he did, he prayed the following prayer of blessing for their mission:

> Almighty Father, Who wilt hear the prayer of them that love Thee, we pray Thee to be with those who brave the heights of Thy heaven and who carry the battle to our enemies. Guard and protect them, we pray Thee, as they fly their appointed rounds. May they, as well as we, know Thy strength and power, and armed with Thy might may they bring this war to a rapid end. We pray Thee that the end of the war may come soon, and that once more we may know peace on earth. May the men who fly this night be kept safe in Thy care, and may they be returned safely to us. We shall go forward trusting in Thee, knowing that we are in Thy care now and forever. In the Name of Jesus Christ. Amen.[1]

Two and a half hours later, three B-29s lumbered into the air, taking off from airstrips built by the Japanese army a few years earlier. Though the war itself did not officially end for another nine days, Captain Downey's prayer that "the end of the war may come soon" began to be answered the moment the lead airplane, piloted by Colonel Paul Tibbets, dropped its payload over the Japanese city of Hiroshima. In a blinding flash of light, the exploding bomb killed eighty thousand people instantly and ushered in the nuclear age. Three days later the squadron flew a second mission over Nagasaki with similar results.

William Downey's role in the bombings of Hiroshima and Nagasaki went beyond his prayers blessing the missions. Long before the bombs were dropped, the chaplain served as spiritual leader to the 509th during grueling months of training in the high desert base near Wendover, Utah. Colonel Tibbets looked to Downey to keep up morale by serving as a combination of pastor and cheerleader to a group of men who, for the most part, had little use for formal religion. Though he never flew a mission, Downey's presence and steadying influence helped make possible the top-secret mission of the first atomic squadron.

On the surface, Downey's role appears to be the ultimate conflict of interest. How could he, a man of the cloth, a servant of God, request God's blessing on missions that resulted in the deaths of hundreds of thousands of people? Isn't God in the business of life, not death? Reading Downey's prayer, I find myself wondering what the Lord Himself must have thought as He heard the words. The city of Nagasaki had one of the largest Christian populations of any city in Imperial Japan.[2] What about the prayers for protection rising from its residents every night?

I don't know. The more I think about it, the more overwhelmed I feel by the intense irony of a prayer of divine blessing over a mission of death. Part of me wants to indict God, to blame Him for not preventing the events that result in wars and suffering and fear that never ends. Wars result from truly human actions. In a sense, the first war broke out shortly after the world was formed. It wiped out one-fourth of the world's recorded population. You can read about it in chapter 4 of Genesis. It's the story of Cain killing his brother, Abel. I know it doesn't qualify as a war in the true sense of the word, but when the world's population consists of a single family, the death of one member makes a major impact. God didn't make Cain hate his brother any more than He causes any person to hate another. Jesus told us to love one another (see John 13:34). How can we blame Him when a man like Hitler kills six million people based on race? Nor does God find pleasure in one nation enslaving entire populations because it possesses the military might to do so. What choice do nations have when other nations use force to further the cause of evil, except to resist with greater force?

What exactly would we have God do to make wars and violence impossible? He could force us to love one another. Perhaps He could make it physically impossible for us to do anything other than honor life and treat others with dignity and respect. I guess He could send an army of angels to put us in headlocks and give us noogies and not let us go until we solemnly swear to never, ever become angry with another person again. In short, God could force us to do the very things He already told us to do. Instead, we ignore His commands and blame Him when death rains down from the sky. We refine cruelty to an art form and then wonder why God allows it to continue.

Don't Just Take My Word for It
The question of evil and suffering has plagued people since time began. We wonder why God allows bad people to harm and kill other people. But is that the real issue? Read Mark 7:20-23. These verses describe the effects of sin on the human heart. What is the real source of rape and murder and wars and other needless acts of violence? How could God prevent these evils acts from overflowing onto the pages of human history? Could He do this while still giving human beings the freedom to either obey or reject the Lord? If you answered yes, how? If you answered no, why?

There's more to the story than this. Read Matthew 5:9. What does it mean to "work for peace"? Why do you think God tells us to do this? How does this fit into your calling to follow Jesus?

> 23

Long Live the King

Elvis Aaron Presley died on August 16, 1977. On each anniversary of his death, newspapers and the evening news dredge up stories about the King of Rock and Roll, especially around my home in central Indiana. The King died less than two months after his final concert at Indianapolis's Market Square Arena. No one knew it would be the last time Elvis would perform live. If we had, someone would have filmed the event. Instead, we now have to satisfy ourselves with Elvis impersonators for the live Elvis experience.

When I heard Elvis was dead, I thought of the King as the old, overweight, over-the-hill performer my mother talked about a lot. My mother loved Elvis. When she was sixteen, she saw him in concert at a county fair in the metropolis of Duncan, Oklahoma. From that point forward she never missed him when he performed nearby. My sisters and I never went with her. Come to think of it, I don't think we were ever invited. My mother didn't want us to see her scream and faint and do what any self-respecting fan does in the presence of rock-and-roll royalty.

Reading stories about the end of Elvis's life, I've wondered if perhaps the King might have been happier if he'd never been crowned. At the time of his death, he struggled with depression and an addiction to prescription drugs. He thought his best days were behind him. Die-hard fans still lined up to hear him perform live, but he hadn't had a hit record in years. People called him a pioneer of rock and roll, but he no longer shaped the face of popular music. Even so, his fame made him a virtual prisoner. Over time he became more and more reclusive and his habits more eccentric. His weight ballooned as his dependence on drugs increased. Yet no one would cut off his supply. Who could say no to Elvis?

If he had never walked into the Sun Records studios in Memphis, the end might have been different. Elvis the truck driver or Elvis the accountant or Elvis the schoolteacher who went to college on the GI Bill after returning from the army might today be Elvis the man making the most of his retirement. Women wouldn't have thrown themselves at him because ordinary guys living ordinary lives usually don't have groupies. His marriage might have lasted until death did them part. Today Elvis could be an eccentric old grandfather who enjoys nothing more than singing for his grandchildren. His audience might moan and groan and laugh, but I can't help but think such a performance would give him greater pleasure than any concert he ever gave.

Elvis the King performed around the world, shook hands with presidents, made small talk with the giants of the entertainment industry, and hung out with the Beatles. He became a legend, and, like most legends, he left before his time. At the end of his life, with all his fame, all his riches, all the girls and parties and drugs, he died an unhappy man lying facedown next to a toilet.

I wish Elvis's story was unique, but it isn't. Recently news broke that another celebrity entered rehab. After reaching the pinnacle of success, after tasting fame and riches and all the things the rest of us can only dream of, she turned to drugs and alcohol to help her cope with her daily misery. Record contracts and movie deals and throngs of adoring fans weren't enough. Now she's trying to get control of her life once again in a drug rehab facility. This news came in the same week NBC devoted several hours of prime-time programming to newly discovered secret tapes made by the late Princess of Wales. In them she describes the living hell that was her life, trapped in a marriage to a man who loved another woman. Juxtaposed against images of her fairy-tale wedding, we hear her cries for love and happiness. Although she was adored around the world, the princess's life never quite measured up to happily ever after. She developed an eating disorder and sank so low that she even attempted suicide. After she died in a car accident, the world mourned her death and wondered if she ever truly found happiness.

As I stand back and reflect on the lives of Elvis and the high-profile celebrity in rehab and the tragic princess, I can't help but wonder why success doesn't bring happiness. In case you think these three may be isolated cases, scan through the news over the next few days. Listen as the rich and famous talk about their past or current battles with drugs and alcohol and depression. This isn't just a twenty-first-century problem either; read Ecclesiastes 2:1-26 for a similar story. Why don't fame and fortune and pleasure and power make us happy? If they can't, what can?

Don't Just Take My Word for It

Read Ecclesiastes 5:10-17. Why do you think God would design us in such a way that we will never be able to find happiness in wealth or pleasure or anything else this world has to offer? What does this say about the physical universe and our place in it? What is God trying to tell us through this?

I know this isn't an easy question, but don't give up too quickly. Think this through. Think about all that this world has to offer. Look at your own desires and the things you want. What do you hope to find in them? Don't limit yourself to material goods. Look ahead to your future. What do you hope to achieve in life? If all of your hopes and dreams and long-range plans come true, then what? How do they look in light of Ecclesiastes?

I don't want to end this on a down note, so read Philippians 3:7-11. What makes the difference between a meaningless life and one that brings joy? So what about you? What do you want out of life? What will it cost you to reach it? Will the price be worth it in the end?

> 24

Dr. Doolittle's Dream Comes True

It may be the greatest scientific breakthrough since the invention of microwave popcorn. Researchers at the Institute of Technology and Biosystems Engineering in Braunschweig, Germany, announced they can now interpret what a cow means when it moos. Engineers recorded seven hundred different sounds from twenty cows, ran them through computer software developed for the project, and can now tell with 90 percent accuracy whether a moo means "I'm hungry" or "I'm thirsty" or "I smell my late uncle on your breath."

The institute hopes to develop a fully functioning call recognizer, which will turn animal vocalizations into text messages. Their website already features a photograph of a cow with the caption, "Speaking Animal."[1] When you click on her, she speaks. She says very clearly, "Moo." Unfortunately, the website doesn't tell you what the cow means by this. But rest assured, she is talking. I clicked on the picture several dozen times, and it always said in an unmistakable cow voice, "Moo."

The sound so moved me that I copied it to my hard drive and made it my e-mail alert. When I hear her moo, I know the cow in my computer is telling me, "You've got mail."

Computer cow translators are only the tip of the iceberg in the exciting field of animal vocalization. A Japanese company already offers the BowLingual. For $99.95 on sale this dog collar records your dog's barks, interprets them, and turns them into a text message you can read. The company is marketing the BowLingual as a toy, but its release was delayed in the United States because its inventors had trouble distinguishing the words, "I plan to bite you if you don't stop bugging me" from other, less menacing sounds. But it is available now at retailers across the country. I don't need a BowLingual for my dachshund. He talks all the time, and when a human male between the ages of thirteen and nineteen is around, every sound means, "Leave while you still have an ankle."

Translation devices for other species can't be far behind. I'm sure someone somewhere will develop a talking collar for cats (where every sound means, "I tolerate you"), birds ("Wake up, it's 5 AM"), horses ("Get off my back"), and teenage boys ("Feed me"). And they will sell. Like baseball players to a cornfield in Iowa, when animal vocalization translators hit the market, customers will come. It sounds like a bargain to pay less than $100 to finally hear a dog's pledge of love and devotion with our own ears. Yet I can't help but think of all we will lose when the mystery is gone and every bark can be understood. I would hate to find out that all those sounds I understood to be expressions of devotion from my dog really mean, "I wish I was outside chasing squirrels."

I don't know how sales have gone for the cow translator, but sales of the BowLingual are brisk. Hundreds of thousands have sold since its release. *Time* magazine named it one of the coolest inventions of 2002.[2] No one will take it too seriously because the dog's vocabulary will be limited to two hundred preset phrases based on its mood, yet everyone will want to have one. If you have a dog, just reading this probably makes you want one.

In spite of the invention of the BowLingual and the cow translator, quality conversations between humans and animals are still impossible. The gulf between us is too great. Contrary to everything you learned from watching *The Lion King* ninety-seven times a day when you were five, animals are not little people dressed in fur.

Another communication gap confronts us—one between God and us. Isaiah 55:8 declares, "'My thoughts are completely different from yours,' says the LORD. 'And my ways are far beyond anything you could imagine.'" God's thoughts and ways are so beyond us that trying to understand them on our own is tantamount to trying to teach your goldfish calculus. Yet from the beginning of time, God has continually opened lines of communication between Himself and human beings. He didn't leave us in the dark. Instead, He reached out to men and women and carried on a conversation with them. Check out two examples in Genesis 15:1-20 and Luke 1:26-38.

We take these conversations for granted, yet stop and think for a moment about what God had to do to make them possible. He is the Sovereign Lord of the universe; human beings are fragile creatures made out of dust. The difference goes beyond the Creator/creation gap. The human race has lived in a constant state of rebellion against God since the moment Adam and Eve sinned in the garden. We run away from God; He chases after us. Romans 3:11 tells us that no one seeks God, yet He seeks us. He does so because He loves us and wants to know us personally (see Romans 5:8).

Don't Just Take My Word for It

God wants to know us and us to know Him. Yet He usually doesn't send an angel to knock on our door, nor does His voice boom down from heaven telling us what we need to hear. How does the God we cannot see with our eyes or hear with our ears communicate with ordinary people like us today? Check out 1 Corinthians 2:9-16. What has God given us? What does it mean to have the mind of Christ? Why would God give us His Spirit and allow us to know the mind of Christ?

Now let's get a little more personal. God's Spirit dwells in us. The passage above tells us that God speaks to us through His Spirit, and His Spirit allows us to understand God's thoughts. Read John 16:5-15. We find God's thoughts in His Word, the Bible. Has this been your experience? Has God reached down to communicate with you through the Bible? Write down some things He has told you.

If all this is true, if God has reached down to communicate with you, what should you do? If people will shell out 100 bucks to try to know what is going through the mind of their cocker spaniel, how much effort should you put out to understand the thoughts of God?

> 25

Miracle or Statistic?

NASA kicked off 2004 by landing two robotic rovers on the surface of Mars. Scientists at NASA and the Jet Propulsion Laboratory broke out in loud cheers and even tears when the first images from the rovers came back to Earth.[1] A few scattered images of a rocky landscape probably won't send chills down your spine or mine, but for the space agency that watched one Martian probe after another disappear without a trace, January 3 and 24, 2004, were red-letter days. Two-thirds of all international missions to Mars have failed, and only three previous spacecrafts have successfully landed on the Red Planet. As recently as ten days before the first Mars Exploration Rover touched down, the British probe Beagle 2 descended toward Mars and was never heard from again.

The latest mission to Mars was initiated for the same reason every probe heads toward Mars: to find signs of life.[2] The twin Mars Exploration Rovers are basically little robot geologists. They cruised around for a few months examining rocks while searching for evidence of water. Water and life go hand in hand. At least they do on Earth. Scientists hope they do on Mars as well.

Neither rover ran into the little green men that made Mars famous. Our illusions of life on such a grand scale there were shattered long ago. NASA wasn't even looking for live bacteria. The best it hoped to find was some evidence that microscopic life lived on Mars in the ancient past. To do that, the robot geologists analyzed rocks with magnets and microscopic imagers and alpha particle X-ray spectrometers, whatever those may be. But the best part of the twin MERs, the one thing that makes this whole mission worth the hundred-million-dollar price tag, is the 3-D pictures the probes radioed back to Earth. Mars in 3-D—it doesn't get any better than that.

Unfortunately, every mission to Mars chips away a little more of the charm the planet once held. Italian priest Pietro Secchi looked through a telescope 128 years ago and saw lines running across the surface of Mars. A year later Giovanni Schiaparelli published a map of the Red Planet that included the straight lines Secchi first observed. He called them *canali*, which means "channels." But most people didn't bother with the translation. They dropped the *i* from the end of the word, and the Martian canals were born.[3] In 1895 astronomer Percival Lowell wrote a book on Mars in which he stated that the canals were evidence that an advanced race of beings once lived there. They dug the canals in a last-ditch effort to save their water-starved planet. His book can still be found online at www.wanderer.org/references/lowell/Mars/. Unlike H. G. Wells' *War of the Worlds* and Ray Bradbury's *Martian Chronicles*, Lowell's book wasn't meant to be fiction. He honestly believed Martians once existed, although in his mind they were not little or green. Lowell believed the average Martian was at least three times the size of an earthling with twenty-seven times the muscle mass and power.

Of course, we now know that Lowell was wrong. Scientists are still tracing the channels, but only in the hope of finding a place where water might have flowed and life might have existed hundreds of millions of years ago.

The search goes on, but not just out of the natural, human longing for knowledge. The human race keeps looking for signs of life on Mars and beyond in hopes of finding some clues to why any life exists at all. As Philip Morrison, nuclear scientist and founder of the Search for Extra-Terrestrial Intelligence radio telescope project, puts it, finding any trace of life on another world would change life from a miracle to a statistic.[4]

Therein lies the great mystery that scientists have not yet been able to unlock. The question that has haunted humanity since the beginning of time is not whether life exists on other planets, but why life exists at all. Jean-Paul Sartre called it the first great philosophical question: Why does anything exist rather than nothing? The more science discovers about the nature of the universe, the louder the question becomes and the less equipped science is to offer a plausible answer.

Knowing that the Lord God created the heavens and the earth tells us how the universe came into existence, but it still doesn't answer the question of why. It simply moves it to a different scale. We're left wondering why God would create the physical universe. What prompted Him to one day utter the words, "Let there be light" (Genesis 1:3)? Nothing compelled Him to create. He is God. He can do or not do anything He wants. When we look around at the mess the human race has made of part of His creation, the question grows even louder. Isaiah 46:10 tells us that God knows the end from the beginning, which means He knew how the human race would turn out. He also knew the price He would pay to bring us back to Himself. Why then would He make us? Why would He create the heavens and the earth?

Don't Just Take My Word for It

Read Psalm 19:1-6. What do these verses say about the purpose of the universe? Now turn to Psalm 8 and read it. Compare these psalms with Revelation 4:11. Based on these three passages, why does the physical universe exist? The universe doesn't just include the sun and the stars and distant planets. You and I are part of it. God made us as well. Why, then, do we exist? What purpose did God have in making us? How does your life need to change in order for you to pursue His purpose?

Science continues to search for an answer to how life came about, but the Bible gives us the why. If we don't understand and live the why, it doesn't matter if we know the how.

> 26

God Made Flesh

I'm writing this while sitting in the waiting area of one of the diagnostic areas of a hospital. A commercial for a psychic hotline is blaring on the television hanging on the wall. On one side of me an old man is trying to catch a few winks. I don't know how he can sleep. These chairs are hardly made for sitting, much less sleeping, and that distinctive hospital smell permeates the air. There's nothing quite like the smell of a hospital. I'm just here waiting. One of my family members is back behind the mystery door somewhere. Occasionally someone emerges from behind the door and calls out the name of whoever gets to go behind the door next. I'd rather not find out what's back there. I'd rather wait.

Country music videos have now replaced the psychic hotline commercial. No one is watching the television. I could probably get away with switching the channel to the highlights of last night's baseball games. But the Yankees didn't play last night, and I can't quite bring myself to break the unwritten rule of waiting rooms across the country: Don't change the channel on the television. Just sit and wait and endure whatever happens to flash across the screen. Most people in rooms like this don't care about what is on television. They care more about the person behind the mystery door or what will happen to them once they cross over to the other side. Lives change as a result of what happens behind that door.

I've almost worked up the nerve to change the channel. Almost. Not quite. I'm still waiting. I'd rather watch the people. The old man keeps sinking lower and lower in the chair. His head just rocked back. He should start snoring any moment now. A new crop of people is slowly replacing those who were in the room when I first walked in thirty minutes ago. A Boogie Bass commercial is about to push me over the edge.

I'm still waiting. And waiting and waiting. I'm not just waiting for my family member to come out from the other side of the mystery door. I'm waiting to leave for vacation. We were supposed to leave this morning. Sharp pains in the middle of the night changed all of that. And that's what strikes me as I sit and wait and wonder why anyone would buy the Boogie Bass compact disc. All of the plans we make hang in a precarious balance. No one knows what tomorrow may hold. We don't know what pains may strike or what surprises may drop on us and change every plan we've made. Life is anything but predictable, no matter how much we pretend otherwise.

As I sit here, my favorite verse keeps popping into my head. I don't know why it is my favorite. Some people find it depressing. You can read it in Ecclesiastes 7:14: "Enjoy prosperity while you can. But when hard times strike, realize that both come from God. That way you will realize that nothing is certain in this life." I like the way the *New International Version* puts the first part: "When times are good, be happy; but when times are bad, consider: God has made the one as well as the other." When times are good, be happy. That's easy. But sitting here listening to an infomercial for the Boogie Bass CD while I wonder what the doctor will say when he walks out, I'm not exactly happy. I don't know yet if this day will qualify as good or bad.

That's what makes life so hard. God doesn't make any guarantees about our futures beyond the promise that when we follow Christ by faith, we will go to heaven when we die. Anything can happen between right now and the moment we walk through the pearly gates. Some days will be good. Others will be bad. Ecclesiastes 7:14 tells me both come from God.

Don't Just Take My Word for It

Why do you think God allows us to live with such uncertainty? Why doesn't He smooth out the bad times and flood our days with good? Why does He leave us sitting in hospital waiting rooms, wondering if we will spend the next couple of days on the beach or sitting beside a hospital bed?

For me the answer lies in 2 Corinthians 5:6-10. Read it and see if you agree. These verses tell me this world of waiting rooms is not my home. I don't belong here. Neither do you. Our home is in heaven. When life in this world takes a turn for the worse, it only makes us more anxious to go home.

But I don't think that's the only reason. Across the room from me sits a woman who can't stop crying. She's waiting for her turn to go behind the mystery door. I know what I am supposed to do as soon as I finish writing this. God wants me to go over to her and pray with her. I don't know what to say to make her stop crying. Probably nothing would help. That doesn't matter. I believe God wants to work through me to reassure this woman that He hasn't forgotten her.

I've got to go and let her know that God cares about what is going on in her life. I wonder if anyone would notice if I change the channel on my way back to my seat?

Section Three

TRYING TO HOLD ON

God has made everything beautiful for its own time.
He has planted eternity in the human heart,
but even so, people cannot see the whole scope
of God's work from beginning to end.

—ECCLESIASTES 3:11

There's an old saying that goes like this: "When you get to the end of your rope, tie a knot and hold on." Sometimes life feels like holding on to a knot at the end of a rope while dangling over a cliff.

At other times, life feels like holding on to the edge of our seats during game seven of the World Series with our team ahead ten to zero. Exciting. Breathless. Holding on to the edge of our seats in life is the ultimate experience.

Or life can feel like holding on to the hand of someone we love as we walk through the mall together, talking, laughing, and having a good time. We hold on and hope the moment will last forever.

Every once in a while life feels like trying to hold on to the end of the leash of a wild wiener dog chasing after a cat. Charging forward. Out of control, except for the leash we hold in our hands. We want to let go, but we have to keep holding on.

Life with Christ is about holding on. He can be the ultimate thrill or the rope that keeps us from falling over the edge of a cliff. He can be the One who loves us more than our minds can comprehend or the leash that keeps life from completely slipping out of our hands. We sometimes forget that our grip stays firm because He is the One holding on to us.

> 27

What Do You Want from a Dog?

What do you want from a dog? It's a fair question. You know we all want something. Why else would we let an animal that eats its own vomit lick us in the face? On the day we go down to the Daisy Hill Puppy Farm to pick one out, we have a pretty good idea what we want. So what about you? What do you want from a dog?

If you're like most people, you probably want a dog that will be loyal and faithful and true. You want a dog like the two in that Disney movie that came out a few years ago. Somehow these two dogs got lost—I mean, really lost. They ended up stranded in the mountains a couple of hundred miles from their family. Oh yeah, they also had a cat with them, but the cat was just along for the ride. The dogs—they were the real heroes. Nothing could stand in their way in their relentless drive to get back home. They crossed rivers, climbed mountains, fought grizzly bears and mountain lions, endured rainstorms and hailstorms and snowstorms and a couple of earthquakes and

Hurricane Andrew and a meteor shower and a full-fledged invasion by aliens. Nothing could stop them until they found their way back home. That's what I want from a dog: loyalty.

And unconditional love. You want your puppy to love you, and he better not be shy about showing it. What am I saying? I've never known a dog that was shy about showing affection. The moment you walk in the room they run around in circles, almost delirious from the joy of seeing you. They bark and jump and dart right to your lap and start licking your face. Sure, it's annoying—and more than a little messy. But you put up with it because a big slobbery hello is just a dog's way of showing how much he loves you.

So what else do you want from a dog? Loyalty. Love. Most of us also want our dog to protect us from bad guys and make us feel better when we are feeling blue and be our friend when all others act like they hate us. We want our dog to be there for us when we need him, but he can't be too needy. After all, we have lives. He doesn't. He needs to patiently wait for us to make time for him without becoming too demanding. When he starts getting on our nerves, he better make some space. A dog doesn't mind. If he is anything, he is understanding. And accepting. And warm and cuddly.

That's what I want from a dog.

But I can't help but think as I look over my list how similar it looks to another list I could make. I hope you don't think I'm crazy, but aren't these the very same things we want from God? I know God isn't a dog, and none of us would be crazy enough to act like He were, but my expectations for the Creator of the universe aren't that different from what I want from the dachshund who sleeps next to the washing machine. Are yours?

Think about it for a moment. Don't we want God to be loyal and loving and faithful and true? We want Him to protect us and make us feel better when we are down and be the one true friend who will never leave us or abandon us. God will be there when we need Him. We assume this every time we pray. Even though we sometimes go days at a time without really thinking about Him or spending any quality time with Him, deep down inside we expect Him to understand. After all, life moves pretty fast. God knows this. He understands.

So what do we really want: God or a warm puppy?

Don't Just Take My Word for It

Confusing God with a furry mammal isn't as odd as you might think. Check out chapter 32 of Exodus. Moses had just led the children of Israel out of their slavery in Egypt and set them on a course toward a land God had promised to give them. Before they could go to the land, they first had to make a stop at Mount Sinai so God could tell these people how He wanted them to live. While Moses was up on the mountain taking dictation from God, the people got restless. They finally decided Moses must be dead. They went to his brother, Aaron, and demanded that he give them a god they could get a handle on. Listen to what he did:

Aaron said, "Tell your wives and sons and daughters to take off their gold earrings, and then bring them to me."

All the people obeyed Aaron and brought him their gold earrings. Then Aaron took the gold, melted it down, and molded and tooled it into the shape of a calf. The people exclaimed, "O Israel, these are the gods who brought you out of Egypt!"

When Aaron saw how excited the people were about it, he built an altar in front of the calf and announced, "Tomorrow there will be a festival to the LORD!" (Exodus 32:2-5)

That last sentence is pretty crazy. The people planned to throw a party for the Lord by dancing around a golden cow. Why did they do that? The God they encountered at Mount Sinai didn't fit the god they wanted. They wanted one who was a little more predictable, a little easier to control, a god who would let them do what they wanted without zapping them with lightning bolts. Read the rest of Exodus 32 to hear God's response to all of this.

So, what do you really want from God? Be honest. List at least five things you expect from Him. Most of us never say these things out loud or write them down, but the thoughts still lurk in the back of our minds. So be honest with God. He already knows what you think. Be honest with yourself. What do you really want from God?

Even more important, what if God never does any of these things you want? What if He leaves you wondering where He is and what He is doing? Will you still follow Him? The people standing at the foot of the mountain in Exodus 32 had to wrestle with that question. They made the wrong choice. Read the first two chapters of Job. He faced the same decision, but he made the right choice. What about you? If God doesn't meet your expectations, will you still follow Him?

Is He really what you want from God?

> 28

Keeping the Fifth Commandment

When I was fourteen, my best friend, Alan, asked me to go with him on his family vacation. The family part was pretty much lacking from this trip because his brothers and sisters were either off at college or old enough to have good excuses not to go. Alan was desperate because spending a week alone with his parents in the small confines of a 1972 Plymouth Fury was only slightly less horrifying than having wisdom teeth cut out without anesthesia. So I went. It was either that or stay at home and watch *The Price Is Right*. Cable didn't exist when I was fourteen. But if I had known the horrors I would see on that trip, I would have turned and run rather than step foot in their car. To this day, the images of what I saw still cause me to break out in a cold sweat and thank God those adults in the front seat weren't my parents.

The horror came about halfway through the trip. We'd spent most of the day at the swimming pool. That in and of itself can be frightening enough. The combination of swimming pools and parents can be deadly. But we escaped the place without incident, since Alan and I were too busy embarrassing ourselves trying to get the attention of the eighteen-year-old blonde lifeguard, who didn't look at us even once through her dark sunglasses. After ninety-seven failed attempts, including one or two fake drownings, we gave up, found Alan's mom and dad, and talked them into leaving to go find something to eat. We went to our respective dressing rooms, changed into street clothes, and met back at their car in the parking lot to go off in search of pizza.

Then it happened, the single greatest act of child mortification I've ever seen. As we drove down the highway, Alan's dad rolled down his window, reached down under his seat, and pulled out a wet athletic supporter. He then proceeded to HANG IT ON HIS SIDE CAR MIRROR TO DRY! That's right. A wet athletic supporter flapped in the wind on the side of the car in full view of God and everyone in broad daylight. Alan's mom and dad carried on a normal conversation, as though everyone hangs wet athletic supporters on their car's side mirrors! They didn't notice Alan and me diving to the floorboard in the backseat or Alan praying, "Oh, God, please, make it stop." To them, nothing could be more normal than driving down the road with an athletic supporter hanging off the side of their car. Alan's dad finally pulled it back inside, not because he knew he was embarrassing his son, but because he was afraid the burst of wind from the trucks in the other lane might make it fly off.

All parents embarrass their children. I know. I am a parent with three teenage daughters. Late at night my wife and I sit down with a pad and paper and plot out what we can do the next day to make our children hope they were switched at birth with some really cool parents who must exist somewhere on this planet. Embarrassing children is just what we do. It's our job. And I, for one, enjoy it.

At some point all parents will embarrass their children. Or disappoint them. Or anger them. Or make them wish they had been raised by wolves. Yet in the midst of this strange cycle comes this command from God: "Honor your father and your mother, as the LORD your God has commanded you, so that you may live long and that it may go well with you in the land the LORD your God is giving you" (Deuteronomy 5:16, NIV). Even though God first addressed this commandment to the ancient Israelites in the Old Testament, He still expects us to obey these words today. Listen to what Paul said:

> Children, obey your parents because you belong to the Lord, for this is the right thing to do. "Honor your father and mother." This is the first of the Ten Commandments that ends with a promise. And this is the promise: If you honor your father and mother, "you will live a long life, full of blessing." (Ephesians 6:1-3)

Here's where the whole parent-child relationship gets a little dicey. We already know we're supposed to obey our parents. That's not news. But the Bible doesn't just tell us to obey. God tells us to honor our parents. Showing honor means showing them courtesy and respect, and not just to their faces. The word also means we are to speak well of our parents to other people. The fact that they do things from time to time that make our faces turn eighteen shades of red doesn't matter. A commandment is a commandment. We're supposed to honor our mothers and fathers.

This doesn't mean you will always agree with your parents or the things they do. They're sinners like the rest of us. There will be times our parents do things that dishonor God and offend other people. Honoring your mother and father doesn't mean blindly accepting everything they do as the right course of action. Yet we still must show them the honor and respect God says they deserve. When we do this, even when it is difficult, we honor and please Him (see Colossians 3:20).

Don't Just Take My Word for It

Read Matthew 7:7-11. What name does Matthew use in reference to God? How does Matthew compare God to an earthly parent? Compare this passage to Psalm 103:13-14. Now read 1 John 4:20-21. How is your relationship with your parents connected to your relationship with God? What does your relationship with your parents say about your relationship with God?

That's why all this matters. The fact that God is called our Father means our attitude toward Him is directly related to our attitude toward our earthly parents. All of our talk about loving God and holding on to Him rings hollow in God's ears if we treat our parents like dirt. We honor God as we honor our mom and dad and submit to their authority without complaining.

For better or worse, your parents are your parents. Come up with one or two ways today to honor God by honoring them.

> 29

Whatever the Cost

Roy Moore, chief justice of the Supreme Court in Alabama, lost his job over taking a stand for God. When he ran for office, he vowed to uphold the Christian tradition upon which he believed our nation was built. He also made no secret of his plan to have a monument to the Ten Commandments constructed and placed inside the Supreme Court building. Voters liked Moore's straightforward affirmation of Christian values and elected him to serve as the chief justice of their highest court.

Unlike some politicians, Moore kept his campaign promises. After taking office, he personally paid to create a granite replica of the stone tablets Moses carried down from Mount Sinai. He then placed the monument in a prominent place in the state Supreme Court building, just as he said he would when running for office. The building seemed to be the natural place for such a monument considering the fact that the Ten Commandments were one of the earliest written legal codes. Much of England's common law and, by extension, the legal codes of the colonies and later the United States can trace their origins back to Moses.

But the other eight justices on the Alabama Supreme Court did not share Judge Moore's enthusiasm. They believed the monument violated the separation of church and state by endorsing Christianity. A frieze in the justices' courtroom in the United States Supreme Court building includes Moses and the Ten Commandments, but they appear in the midst of other lawgivers throughout history. The Alabama monument stood alone. Judge Moore himself removed any doubt as to the monument's purpose. Over and over he stated that he built it as a testimony to the Judeo-Christian roots of the country and as a call for a return to those values.

When a federal judge ordered the removal of the monument, Judge Moore refused. The drama played out as the lead story of the national evening news as protesters rallied to Moore's side. They called it the latest battle in the culture war and vowed to do all they could to keep the monument in place. In the end they lost. The monument was removed, and Judge Moore lost his job. And, some lamented, God was once again pushed further and further out of public life.

But was He?

Because God is all-powerful, it will take more than the removal of a monument from a court building in Alabama to keep Him silent. Monuments and paintings and displays on courthouse lawns during the holidays don't put Him on display for all to see. Since before the days of Moses, God has chosen to make Himself known through the people who follow Him. There's a cliché that says, "You're the only Jesus some people will ever see." It may be a cliché, but it is true. You and I reveal God to the world.

When we look at Judge Moore's story from that perspective, we realize that the judge who was willing to take a stand, even if it meant losing his job, said far more about God than the granite monument did. He wanted to honor God and acknowledge the role He played in the foundation of the laws we take for granted. When push came to shove, he wouldn't back down. He is a true believer, which is perhaps what his opponents found so disturbing. We live in a time when few people believe in absolute truth. We're taught we should be open to every idea, every lifestyle, every concept of God and truth and right and wrong. Moore wouldn't play that game but instead insisted that God's Word is absolutely true. The piece of granite was just a symbol. The real message came from Moore himself.

Don't Just Take My Word for It

Read 1 Kings 22:10-28. To understand the passage you'll need to know a few details. Ahab, the king of Israel, worshipped idols and married the queen of idol worshippers, a woman named Jezebel. The longer Ahab sat on the throne, the more the worship of false gods like Baal spread among the people who were supposed to be God's unique possession. Needless to say, God wasn't pleased. Yet few people would speak out against Ahab. Instead, most just went along with him, even those who were supposed to be God's spokesmen.

Micaiah refused to play this game. Like Judge Moore, Micaiah took a stand for the Lord. How is the outcome of the story in 1 Kings 22 similar to the end of Judge Moore's story? Is this the outcome you expect when you think about someone taking a bold stand for God? Why or why not? Holding on to Christ means clinging to His truth and standing up for it, even when no one wants to listen.

Read 2 Corinthians 5:11-21. What role does the passage say you and I and every believer fill in God's plan? What does verse 20 call us? Ambassadors don't represent themselves. They represent the views of the one who sent them. That means they don't try to conform to the nation in which they serve. Instead, they speak for the country they represent, even when those views aren't popular. How well do you represent the One who sent you? How can you take a stand for the truth?

> 30

Out of Control

I was minding my own business, scanning across a page of the Bible and looking for words of comfort and joy, when my eyes came across a sentence I haven't been able to forget. It hasn't given me much comfort. Or joy. Not yet at least. Don't get me wrong, this sentence didn't send me reeling into a tailspin of guilt and despair and feelings of worthlessness before God. I didn't come face-to-face with some glaring moral failure in my life. Either would be easier than reexamining the way I'm spending this brief moment of time I call my life. But that's what I've been forced to do since the moment I came across the sentence I cannot forget.

I wish I had never opened this particular translation of the Bible. It lacks the poetic flow of some of the older versions. I like poetic flow. I find it easy to ignore. I tried moving on to other parts of the Bible. Maybe, I kept telling myself, some other sentence or story would set me free. But I *know* God is trying to tell me something through these nineteen words penned by a guy named Paul a long time ago.

Imagine that. God speaking to a guy like me. He told me

that "my life is worth nothing unless I use it for doing the work assigned me by the Lord Jesus" (Acts 20:24). Maybe these words shouldn't bug me. But they do. Listen closely to what they say. Long ago, long before I was ever thought of, long before my great-grandparents were even thought of, God came up with a plan for my life. He had designed the whole flow of human history and knew where He wanted me to fit into it. As He looked it all over, He came up with specific assignments for me. Then He gave me a choice: I can either waste my life, or I can use it doing His assignments. But it's not just me He's talking about. The same holds true for you and for every follower of Christ.

All this sounds great, except for one little detail: Don't we have any say in the matter? What if God's assignments consist of stuff we're no good at or stuff we don't want to do?

When I think of assignments, I think of Mrs. Perkins' ninth grade English class. Man, I hated that class. All day every day we went over sentence structure and parts of speech and all that boring grammar garbage we'd had since first grade. About halfway through the semester, I started raising my hand every day and asking why we had to have so much English and when we would use it. Once or twice Mrs. Perkins tried giving me an answer, but usually she just gave us homework that consisted of writing essays and paragraphs and other assignments I couldn't wait to get away from.

What if God gave me a lifetime of doing English assignments?

Wait a minute.

I'm a writer.

My life is basically a long series of English assignments.
But I love being a writer.

I couldn't imagine doing anything else.

So how did God get me to love something I used to hate? The difference isn't that I get paid to do this now. I would write for free. In fact, up until a couple of years ago, I did. Did God just brainwash me, or is something else at work here?

I believe something else is at work. When we come to Christ, we discover who we really are. God made each of us. He is the One who gave us our talents and interests. Sin tries to distort both and cause us to be interested only in ourselves. But when we come to Christ, we are finally able to be who God made us to be. That doesn't just mean avoiding sin and doing good deeds. It also applies to the work Jesus arranged for us to do. Read Ephesians 2:10. This work is inseparably linked to God's gracious act of saving you and me.

Don't Just Take My Word for It

So how do you figure out what God created you to do? Read Psalm 37:3-7. What promise does God make to you in these verses? How could that relate to what we've been talking about? How can delighting in God help you figure out the assignment He has for your life? Here's a hint: When we delight in the Lord, which means loving Him more than anything or anyone, the desires of our hearts stop revolving around the latest fashions or the hottest cars. Instead, God tells us that He will give us what we want more than any other thing because our desires will be wrapped up in Him. At the top of our wish lists will be using our gifts to serve God. The key is discovering what He made us to do and then doing it for Him.

What talents has God given you? What do you love to do? What are you good at? What people has God given you a burden for? How can you put all these together for God's glory? Sometimes the assignments God has for us consist of things we don't know we can do until we try. Look around your church and in your youth group. What opportunities for service do you see? Try them. If you try something and end up hating it and stinking at it, don't worry. Try something else. Remember, when you long to please God with your life, He will make sure you find the work that will.

> 31

Living Without Regrets

Cody wanted to be a preacher when he grew up, just like his dad. Once or twice a week he would climb on top of a chair in the kitchen, pull out a Bible, and give his best sermon on John 3:16. He always used the same Bible verse. It was his favorite. "For God so loved the world," the verse begins, "that he gave his only Son, so that everyone who believes in him will not perish but have eternal life." Cody believed this promise, and he wanted to make sure other people had an opportunity to believe it as well. Standing in the checkout line at the grocery store with his mom or dad, he would ask the clerk, "Do you know Jesus?" He asked his teachers and the other kids on the playground the same question. That's what preachers do, and Cody wanted to be a preacher, just like his dad.

I attended Cody's funeral one snowy January afternoon several years ago. He was eight. Four days earlier, Cody died alone in a tragic accident. I hope I live the rest of my life without seeing another eight-year-old in a casket. His right hand clutched a rope. Cody loved tying knots. His favorite stuffed animal lay beside him, along with his Bible and a picture of his brother.

135

Over two thousand people came through the funeral home in southern Kentucky the night before his funeral. They all heard the same story of how Cody wanted to be a preacher, just like his dad. And they all heard the same question that Cody had asked friends and strangers alike: "Do you know Jesus?"

I can't shake the image of Cody lying in a casket in the front of the funeral home. Deep inside I wished I could disrupt a funeral like Jesus had a habit of doing. Every time Jesus came across a funeral procession, he raised the dead person back to life. More than once he raised a child from the dead and gave that child back to the family. Cody's parents and brother walked away from Cody's grave empty-handed. There would be no miracles on this day.

But in a sense there were. The accident that took Cody's life shook the entire community. As a result, everyone in town heard his story, and everyone in town heard his favorite question: "Do you know Jesus?" Cody didn't wait until he grew up to do what he always wanted to do. Even at eight years of age he was a preacher, just like his dad. He lived his life the way I hope I can live mine: without regrets, without putting off what really matters. Cody lived his life for the One who loved him so much that He gave His one and only Son so that Cody would not perish but have everlasting life.

Still, Cody's parents and extended family will never fully recover from his death. They didn't set foot in his room for months after he died. As a father, I don't know how they ever could. The scars inflicted that cold winter day may never go away. When God created the world, death wasn't part of the picture. Cody's death is a tragedy.

Yet I believe that Cody's story is also a story of triumph. King David prayed in Psalm 39:4, "LORD, remind me how brief my time on earth will be. Remind me that my days are numbered, and that my life is fleeing away." Paul echoed David's sentiments when he told the church in Ephesus, "So be careful how you live, not as fools but as those who are wise. Make the most of every opportunity for doing good in these evil days" (Ephesians 5:15-16). These words describe Cody's brief life. He made the most of every opportunity. He didn't wait to fulfill the dreams God planted in his soul. His life may have been short, but he squeezed everything out of it. When he walked through the gates of heaven, this eight-year-old boy heard God say, "Well done."

Don't Just Take My Word for It

Most of us approach life as though we will never die, as though we have all the time in the world. But we don't. Our time here is limited. Are you doing what you know you ought to do for God? Read James 4:13-17. Pay particular attention to the last verse.

You don't have to wait a lifetime to start living out God's purpose for your life. What do you think God has called you to do? How will you start doing it today? If your life ended tomorrow, would you be able to look God in the eye and say, "I did what You asked me to do"?

> 32

Hands Too Full

Two thousand years ago or so a man came to Jesus with a dilemma. He'd devoted his life to religious activity, yet his life still felt hollow. So he filled the emptiness with stuff—lots of stuff. You name it, he had it. But it wasn't enough. The emptiness wouldn't go away, so he kept looking for something more. You can hear a note of desperation in his words: "Good Teacher, what should I do to get eternal life?" (Mark 10:17). It wasn't an academic question. The guy wasn't conducting a personal poll to discover the most popular path to eternal life among leading rabbis. He desperately needed an answer for himself. The hollowness in his soul had taken its toll. Everything he'd tried so far hadn't worked. He wanted relief. He wanted something more out of life.

That's why he hunted Jesus down. The man came running out of the crowd and fell on his knees in front of Him. With his chest heaving from lack of breath and his heart racing, he spit out his question and prayed for an answer. Jesus' answer was simple: "You know the commandments: 'Do not murder. Do not commit adultery. Do not steal. Do not testify falsely.

Do not cheat. Honor your father and mother'" (Mark 10:19).

"'Teacher,' the man replied, 'I've obeyed all these commandments since I was a child.'" *And it wasn't enough*, he implied without saying. *Now what? Tell me something more.*

Then "Jesus felt genuine love for this man as he looked at him. 'You lack only one thing,' he told him. 'Go and sell all you have and give the money to the poor, and you will have treasure in heaven. Then come, follow me'" (Mark 10:21). Treasure in heaven, life everlasting, everything the man ever dreamed of was his for the taking. All he had to do was sell all his possessions and rid himself of everything in this world that gripped his heart. Then he would be free to follow Jesus.

But the young man walked away sad because he had many possessions. If Jesus had told him to stand on his head and count backward from one million, he might have done it. Adding an activity, no matter how odd it might sound, would have been a small price to pay for something as precious as eternal life. But Jesus didn't tell the man to do more. He called him to less. Have fewer possessions. Do less religious activity. Give stuff away. Leave your life behind. Then follow Me.

The man couldn't bring himself to do what Jesus asked. Isn't it ironic? His hands were so full that he didn't have room for the one thing he really wanted. He couldn't get past the price tags on the items that filled his house. Besides, his chariot was new, the horses Arabian, and the camels and flocks irreplaceable. Give everything away? What about the hard work it took to accumulate all this stuff? It had taken years to buy it and now Jesus wanted him to give it all away in one fell swoop. The thought struck him as absurd, and he walked away rich but empty.

This desperate encounter with Jesus came down to one question: Which do you want more, either Jesus or _____? We don't usually think of this as an either/or decision. We want both/and. Both Jesus and success. Both Jesus and the latest fashions. Both Jesus and a really hot set of wheels. The point of the story isn't that you have to be poor to be a Christian. That misses the mark entirely.

Instead, Jesus' message is simply this: We cannot hold on to Him when our hands are filled with everything else. Saint Augustine said it best: "God wants to give us something, but cannot, because our hands are full—there's nowhere for Him to put it."

Don't Just Take My Word for It

Read Exodus 20:1-20. Jesus quoted part of these verses to the rich guy you just read about. Pay particular attention to verses 3-6. What does God mean when He says, "I, the LORD your God, am a jealous God"? How do we share our affection that should go to God alone?

Keep this idea in your head and turn to Mark 10:28. What does it mean to give up everything to follow Jesus? Now look at your own life. What do you see that fills your hands and keeps them from holding on to Christ? It could be anything— a boyfriend or girlfriend, popularity, or a grudge you don't want to let go of. What should you do now? The rich guy who came to Jesus left Him and went away sad. What a waste. Don't make the same mistake.

> 33

Storybook Romance

It wasn't the best way to start a new life together. The couple never came out and told me they needed to have the wedding while the wedding dress would still fit, but it didn't take me long to catch on. Everything connected with the wedding was rushed. The date, the premarital counseling sessions, the reception plans, everything was stuck on fast-forward. Even after I caught on, I acted as though I was still in the dark. The bride-to-be seemed embarrassed enough by the reality growing within her body without me bombarding her with questions she didn't want to face.

Some people might have questioned why this couple wanted to get married in a church. After all, neither one of them attended church. It wasn't that they were anti-God. If anything, they were ambivalent. The whole religion thing didn't register on their radar as good or bad. But the bride-to-be was my family's favorite waitress at our favorite restaurant. I was the only preacher she knew and the only one she felt she could trust.

Like I said, it wasn't the best way to start a new life together. Therefore I wasn't surprised when the new bride called me less than six months after saying "I do" to tell me he left. "I'm not totally sure, but I think he moved in with an old girlfriend," she told me. She never wanted to walk down the aisle three months pregnant, and she certainly never wanted to be a single mother. My first reaction was anger, not at her, but at the bum she married. (Sorry, did I call him a bum in print?)

Life bottomed out quickly for Karen. With nowhere else to go, she swallowed her pride and moved back in with her mom and dad. The baby kept growing, and Karen started preparing for life as a single mother. She also did something else she'd never done before. She started coming to church. The messages she heard stayed with her. She felt very comfortable sitting in a pew, listening to songs and stories about God. Most of the people in the church knew her. After all, she was everybody's favorite waitress at the best pizza place in the county. A month before the baby was born, Karen made another decision, one that changed her life and her eternal destiny. Rather than just hear stories about God, she crossed the line and asked God to save and forgive her. The next Sunday I baptized her, even though she wasn't sure she would fit in the tank with her very pregnant stomach sticking out.

And so the story had a happy ending after all. God worked all things out for good. He turned the tragedy of a crisis pregnancy into the wonder of a new birth in Christ. The only thing that could have made the story better would have been for her estranged husband to come back home, receive Christ, and live happily ever after with his family.

The first part of the equation came true. A week after Conner came into the world, Karen's husband asked for a second chance. She gave a tentative yes. Before she would act as though everything was wonderful, she wisely told him the two of them would need to go through counseling together. That's when my phone rang again.

The rest of the fairy-tale ending never came to pass. Even after she forgave him for all he had done—the adultery, abandonment, and embarrassment—he eventually walked away. He demanded something Karen could never do. He wanted her to drop the whole Christianity thing. Forced to choose between living with a Christian wife and running back into the fast lane, he chose the latter. No happily ever after for this couple. No last-minute reconciliation. Now Karen is another single mother scraping by to create a life for herself and her son.

Entrusting oneself to God doesn't guarantee a lifetime of blessings and smiles and laughter. Those who think it will miss the point entirely. C. S. Lewis said it best: "If Christianity is untrue, then no honest man will want to believe it, however helpful it might be. If it is true, every honest man will want to believe it, even if it gives him no help at all."[1] It's easy to believe in a God who will make all our dreams come true, a God who will sweep away all our problems and replace them with sunshine and joy. But when life doesn't turn out for the best, when the worst-case scenarios come closer to reality than we ever thought they would, what will we do then?

Karen made her choice. She once told me that the entire experience was worth the pain. Without it, she would never have the two most important things in her life: Jesus and her son, Conner. God didn't make her life perfect, but He did stay true to His promise to never leave her or forsake her. Armed with that, Karen knows she can survive anything this life can throw at her.

Don't Just Take My Word for It

Read chapter 11 of Hebrews. It's known as the Faith Hall of Fame. As you read, underline the name of everyone listed whose life didn't turn out exactly the way that individual wanted. You may have to go to the Old Testament to read a little more of their stories. For example, the first name listed is Abel. You'll find him in Genesis 4. His brother killed him because Abel pleased God; his brother, Cain, didn't.

Look back over the names you've underlined. If so many people trusted God with such amazing faith yet weren't spared heartache and pain and suffering, what can we expect in this life? What do you need to do to prepare yourself for what may lie ahead? What bad things have already happened in your life? How has God used them to shape your life and use you for His purposes?

> 34

Ordinary Day

The alarm went off this morning, and my mind filled with all sorts of things I need to accomplish today. Big things. Important things. Things that can't be put off. Urgent things. Life-and-death things. But nothing so big that I couldn't grab nine more minutes of sleep. And nine more. And nine more. And nine more, until my wife finally complained about me hitting the snooze button over and over and over.

So I drug myself into the shower. As hot water spilled over my head, I thought about everything I need to accomplish. Big things. Important things. Things that can't be put off. But nothing so important that I couldn't spend a little time reading the box scores from last night's games in this morning's paper while eating my bowl of Corn Pops. I know. I'm old. I don't go to the games anymore; I just read about them in the paper. But that's not all I read. I also check out the reviews of the hottest movies, and no one can pick up a paper without reading the comics. At least I can't.

While I was brushing my teeth and combing my hair and making myself presentable to the world, I remembered all the things I need to do today. Big things. Important things. Urgent things. But nothing so urgent that I couldn't spend a little time with Matt and Katie and the rest of my close friends on the *Today* show. They had an interview with an associate of someone who used to work in the White House, along with a segment on how to remove those annoying facial wrinkles without surgery. The star of Hollywood's newest blockbuster stopped by, and they even showed a clip of the movie. And how could I watch *Today* without waiting for Willard Scott to walk out into his front yard to wish a Smuckers Happy Birthday to everyone born before 1904?

I finally made it to my office, which isn't much of an achievement since it sits next to the living room in my house. As I turned on my computer, I was reminded of all the things I need to do today. Big things. Weighty things. Things with eternal significance. But nothing that couldn't wait until after I checked my e-mail. What kind of friend would I be if I didn't answer the people who went to all the trouble of forwarding that sad story about the boy and his pet starfish? And because I was already online, I figured I might as well check out last night's Late Show Top Ten list.

After a little IM conversation with a friend, I'm struck with a shadowy thought of something I needed to do today. It seems like it was something big. Something important. Something urgent. Something with eternal life-or-death significance. But I just can't remember what it might have been. Not that it matters now. Not at the office. Not with deals to close and contacts to make. Business is business, and it can't be put off. Not with a mortgage and the car payment and the orthodontist bills hanging over my head and vacation plans in the works.

I faintly remember needing to do something today. But it is nothing so important that it can't wait until tomorrow.

I know I'm probably the only person in America who loses sight of the important while immersed in the trivial. On second thought, probably not. It is as though the human body comes equipped with a time-waster gene. We don't mean to do it. At least not when we need to get things done. But distractions have a way of grabbing us by the nose, and before we know it we forget what we were trying to accomplish. In the short time it has taken me to write today's devotional, I've gone to get a Vanilla Coke, read an e-mail the e-mail cow announced was in my in-box, checked on my dog who is wrapped up in a blanket asleep in the back of the house, brushed my teeth, and dug through a stack of CDs in search of the perfect writing music. I finally settled on Switchfoot's *Legend of Chin*. It's their first CD and probably their best, although *Beautiful Letdown* is pretty good and I do like *New Way to Be Human* and I also like to listen to Jars of Clay while I write. All of my Jars CDs are old, but so am I, and sometimes I listen to Relient K and here I go again wasting time talking about nothing!

That's the real problem you and I face as we try to walk through this life clinging to the hand of Christ. We're easily distracted. Our intentions may be noble, but our performance is often lacking. Deep down we want our lives to count for something beyond ourselves. We want to spend our time fulfilling God's purposes for our lives. But then the IM chime rings or *Sabrina* reruns come on or we notice our little brother beat our high score on Snood, and the big things we hoped to accomplish, the important things that weighed heavily on our minds, the things that can't be put off are put off until tomorrow and the next day and the next and the next.

Don't Just Take My Word for It

Read Ephesians 5:15-20. What does this passage say about our built-in ability to waste time? Why is this a problem for most of us? Now focus on verse 16. What does it mean to "make the most of every opportunity for doing good"? How does it relate to verse 17? Does knowing what God wants you to do make it easier to use your time wisely? Why or why not? And don't give some lame Sunday school answer. Be honest. What effect does knowing what God wants you to do have on your day-to-day life (not the fantasy life we often live in the land of denial)? Why is this a struggle?

Today, like all days, God will give you the opportunity to do something for Him. It may be something as simple as encouraging a friend who is really down. Or you may have the chance to tell someone how he or she can know Christ personally. Sometimes the tasks God has for us are small; other times they are huge. But everything you do for God lasts forever.

Every day comes down to a choice. You have perhaps sixteen waking hours (maybe twelve on those summer days when you sleep until noon and stay up until midnight). How you use those hours is completely up to you. You can invest them in big things, important things, things that can't be put off, or you can let them slip through your fingers. Here's your challenge for today: Ask God to open your eyes to opportunities for doing good that He has for you today. Then do them. Pretty simple, huh?

> 35

Why Did the Banana Cross the Road?

Bananas may be nature's perfect food. Rich in potassium, low in calories, and high in taste, Americans consume them by the ton. From banana pudding to banana nut bread to frozen chocolate-covered bananas on a stick, you can make almost anything out of them. There are banana splits and banana shakes, banana muffins and New England–style Bananas Foster. You can eat them plain or put them in a fruit salad or mix them into ice cream or, my personal favorite, slice them on top of a bowl of Wheaties. Yummm, the perfect food on top of the perfect breakfast cereal.

But the banana smorgasbord may be coming to an end. Recently published reports warn that bananas may soon go the way of the dodo and the dinosaur. If something isn't done soon, bananas may disappear within ten years. We aren't eating them into extinction. After all, unlike money, they do grow on trees, and those trees spread across the tropics around the world. Therein lies the problem. The vast majority

of banana trees, regardless of location, are virtual carbon copies of one another. The modern banana lacks genetic diversity.
Therefore, any parasite or disease that strikes one tree has the
potential to wipe out the world's supply. Isn't it ironic? The
fruit we eat in a thousand different ways finds itself threatened
by its uniformity.

The banana crisis shouldn't surprise us. Uniformity always
makes a species weaker. The more alike plants or people may
be, the more at risk they actually are. This is especially true
of the human race. Most of us feel threatened by those who
aren't like us. Whether the pigmentation in their skin is different or their ideas run counter to our own or their outlook
on life is just plain strange, diversity makes us uncomfortable.
Variety may be the spice of life, but most people prefer their
life bland. Those strange people with their strange ways of
doing things perplex us. And worse.

In our minds we start deducting IQ points from those who
are different, thinking that anyone who would rather listen to
Toby Keith over Jimmy Eat World can't be playing with a full
deck. If you agree with the preceding statement, you can rest
assured that somewhere a country music fan thinks the same
thing about you. Before long we perceive people's differences
as a threat. If they aren't for us, they must be against us, and if
they aren't like us, they must have some hidden agenda.

So what do we do? We separate ourselves from the weir-
dos and erect barriers to keep the radicals with their radical
ideas at bay. When we do find ourselves in the proximity of
someone who doesn't look or sound or smell like us, we fight
and push and try to either make him exactly like us or stay as

far away from him as possible. Through it all we wonder how anyone could be so blind, so unthinking, so wrong.

Most people see diversity as a threat when in fact it's our greatest strength. God could have made us all alike. He could have given us one skin color and one height and one weight and one way of thinking about the world. If He had wanted, He could have made us all extroverts, and He could have given us all an ear for classic rock and a taste for Italian food. But when He made the human race, He made us all different, unique. Those differences shouldn't threaten us. Quite the opposite. They are the source of our strength. History shows that uniform cultures are most at risk of falling under the spell of tyrants. Freedom and progress demand differences that clash in the marketplace of ideas. Without them we would soon join the banana on the threshold of extinction.

Diversity is especially important in our quest to follow Christ. You and I aren't alone on this journey. Sometimes we think we are. In our minds we picture ourselves walking along with Christ, our hand in His, just the two of us alone on a lonely beach. But we aren't alone. Right now, at this very moment, millions of other Christ followers are spread out across the world on every continent. This group includes people from every race and nearly every nationality with every hue of skin God in His creative imagination chose to create. Our gifts are different, the way we see the world is different, even some of our beliefs are different. Although we all agree on who Jesus is and what He did to save us, the expressions of our faith vary from place to place and person to person.

This is a good thing.

Don't Just Take My Word for It

Read 1 Corinthians 12:12-27. God made us different for a reason. First Corinthians 12 tells us to think of our differences like the differences among the parts of our body. Imagine if your whole body were nothing but one giant eye. School would be just plain creepy with a few hundred giant eyeballs jumping around the halls and bouncing into one another. Or what if your entire body was nothing but a giant nose? That would make life more interesting, especially during cold and flu season. I think our bodies should be nothing but a giant navel. Yep, one big belly button from head to toe (which, of course, we wouldn't have since our heads and toes would be part of the big belly button).

If the thought of a body with only one part sounds absurd, how much more absurd is the thought of the human race all being clones of you? Agent Smith (Hugo Weaving) tried that in *The Matrix Revolutions*, and it didn't work out too well for him. Because God made us all different for a reason, what should your attitude be toward people who look and act completely different from you?

Look back over 1 Corinthians 12:12-27. Even though everyone is different, what one thing do we all need? Or, better said, Who do we all need? Do all of our differences disappear when we become followers of Jesus? Why or why not?

Look around at the other Christians you hang out with. How are you all different? Look beyond the obvious, beyond the external stuff such as hair color and race. What differences do you see that sometimes cause disagreements and arguments? What can you do to make that diversity a strength rather than a weakness? How can the differences be used by God to accomplish His purposes in the world? What would happen if all of these differences disappeared?

You and I might be more comfortable hanging out with people who are exactly like us, but God doesn't share this belief. He made us different for a reason. After all, in the eyes of that guy over there, you are the strange one.

> 36

Simple Words

I guess I'm a little slow or a little naive. When I hear people use words, I assume they mean what they say. That's where I'm having trouble. I can't help but wonder how a certain act of intimacy can be used as an adverb and an adjective describing everything from a hammer to the need to leave a room. But that's how people talk today. I know you hear this stuff in the hallways of your school every day, but I don't get out much. However, the other day these two guys were working on a house under construction next door. I didn't mean to eavesdrop, but my window was open. Here's what they had to say as they discussed one man's need for a hammer:

> Man A: Hand me that procreating hammer.
> Man B: What the procreation are you talking about? Get the procreator yourself, you lazy procreator.
> Man A: Who you calling a procreator, you procreator? Now hand me the procreating hammer.
> Man B: I ain't touchin' that procreating hammer for you, you stupid procreator. Hey, it's quittin' time. Let's get the procreation out of here.

I doubt if either man truly believes the hammer capable of procreation, and yet of all the ways they could describe a hammer, physical intimacy between a man and a woman is the only one these two seemed capable of using. This had to be some hammer. It wasn't a brown hammer or a black hammer or a silver hammer or a claw hammer or a ball-peen hammer or a sledgehammer. This unique combination of steel and wood used to drive nails into walls was a procreating hammer. Procreating, as though the men caught the hammer in the very act. Just to be safe, I checked a dictionary. The men's favorite word was nowhere to be found.

And it's not just the act of procreation that peppers speech. Other bodily functions, body parts, and animals and their offspring also play a prominent role in conversations everywhere from high school hallways to work sites to the silver screen. Feces and procreation seem to be the perfect words to describe everything from great disappointment to overwhelming joy. Others call down curses upon themselves when surprised. I've even heard people ask God to eternally condemn an errant golf shot. At least that's what their words literally mean.

Some believe these words serve a purpose. They think they make us sound grown-up, cool, and maybe a little intimidating to the uninitiated. They help us blow off steam when we're angry. Little boys and girls sneak them with their friends like cigarettes behind a garage, hoping not to slip around their mother and incur the wrath of soap scraped across their teeth. The more we use them, the more ingrained in our vocabulary they become. They slip from the tongue with the greatest of ease. With time, we don't even realize we're using them or give a thought to what they say about our character.

I know, I need to lighten up. People don't really mean what they say. They don't really want the girl spreading rumors to be condemned to a fiery pit for all of eternity. Telling her to go there is just a figure of speech. And apart from Charles Barkley, I've never heard of anyone actually puckering up to a donkey. They're just words. Everybody says them. No one actually means them. It's just the way people talk. No one takes it seriously.

No one, that is, but God.

The book of James says, "If you claim to be religious but don't control your tongue, you are just fooling yourself, and your religion is worthless" (James 1:26). When profanity rains down around us every day, it is hard to keep the words from seeping into our own vocabularies. We hear it in the halls at school, from the other guys on the team, and in the locker room. It comes at us on television and in the movies and in the songs on the radio. If we aren't very, very careful, the words we hear every day will start coming out of our own mouths. That's why James says we must control our tongues. If we don't, everything we say we believe about God and all our talk about following Him is worthless.

Don't Just Take My Word for It

Profanity isn't just a problem for the two guys working on the house outside my window. Many people who claim to be walking hand in hand with Jesus use it as well. Read Ephesians 4:29: "Don't use foul or abusive language. Let everything you say be good and helpful, so that your words will be an encouragement to those who hear them." What do you think this means? How do your favorite expressions fit into this verse? If someone didn't already know you are a Christian, would he be surprised to find out based on the other words he's heard come out of your mouth?

You already know how you are doing in this area. Spend some time talking with God about it. Ask Him to change the words that flow through your mind, the words that come out when you least want them to. You also need to stop sticking those words in your head. Jesus said, "If your hand causes you to sin, cut it off. It is better for you to enter life maimed than with two hands to go into hell, where the fire never goes out" (Mark 9:43, NIV). It's time to take His principle seriously. You don't need to cut off your ears, but if the music you listen to causes you to stumble, get some different music. If the movies you watch cause you to fall, stop watching them. Don't just pray for God's help; take some active steps to clean this junk out of your life. Make a list of stumbling blocks in your life. Now what will you do with them? The answer isn't always simple.

I know, they're just words. No one takes them seriously. But God does. Not using profanity is one of the simplest, most basic steps we can take to show we are serious about walking with Jesus.

> 37

Free Willy

In 1993 Keiko stole the hearts and minds of America with his masterful portrayal of Willy, the killer whale in *Free Willy*. Some critics complained the part did not stretch Keiko dramatically, but most agreed he was the best actor in the film. Shortly after the movie's release, word got out that Keiko shared more with his alter ego, Willy, than anyone dared imagine. He too was an oppressed killer whale. The Mexican amusement park that owned Keiko kept him in a tank far too small for a whale his size. A cry rose up from across the land: Free Willy, er, Keiko.

Three years later humanitarian groups finally raised enough money to start the process. They moved Keiko to a larger park in Oregon where marine biologists started the long process of reintroducing him to the wild. It was no easy task. Keiko was captured in 1979 at the age of two off the coast of Iceland. Life in the pool was all he had known for seventeen years. He knew how to catch a ball on his nose, but he didn't know how to catch a fish . . . unless, of course, someone tossed it to him from the top of a really tall ladder.

From Oregon, Keiko traveled back to Iceland in 1998 where he continued to learn the fine art of doing more than playing the part of a killer whale on film. It took four years and over twenty million dollars, but he finally graduated from whale school. Experts deemed him ready for life in the wild. Willy, er, Keiko, was free at last. Everyone hugged and sang Kum Ba Yah as he swam off into the sunset, or at least they should have.

There was only one small problem. Nobody thought to ask Keiko if he wanted to be free. Researchers released him off the coast of Iceland in hopes he would reunite with his long-lost family pod, and Keiko did. He swam nearly nine hundred miles to a narrow fjord in Norway to find the only family he really cared about: people.

Every day crowds of boats gathered to play with the thirty-foot whale. People didn't have to search for the whale; he looked for them. While most killer whales spend their day eating fish and seals, Keiko preferred swimming with children and rolling over for people to rub his belly. Apparently he flunked the "wild" part of his training to become a wild animal.

Those who visited Keiko in his Norwegian fjord enjoyed the experience until the experts spoke up again. They pointed out that the approaching winter might kill Keiko because he spent his days playing rather than eating or migrating to wherever he was supposed to spend his winter. One leading whale expert went so far as to suggest that it would be more humane to kill Keiko than to wait for his carcass to wash up on shore sometime the following spring.[1] But those who worked so hard to set Keiko free didn't let that happen. They moved him away from the crowds and the ice to a safe home in a protected bay.

Although he'd gone through several years of intensive training on how to catch and eat live fish, Keiko never quite caught on. Every day his handlers fed him 150 pounds of frozen herring. He continued doing tricks for them, although they discouraged him from doing so. But once an entertainer, always an entertainer, and Keiko couldn't help himself. Like McDonalds, he loved to see people smile.

Marine mammal activists working on Keiko's case hoped he would return to the wild someday, up until the day he contracted pneumonia and died in December 2003. Veterinarians worked frantically to save his life, but in the end the millions of dollars spent for his rehabilitation and the hundreds of hours given by volunteers couldn't keep Keiko from dying at least ten years earlier than he should have.[2] Setting Keiko free seemed to be the right thing to do, but he probably would have been better off had he simply been moved to a better park with a larger tank.

Just because something feels right doesn't mean it is. Everyone wanted to see Willy go free at the end of the movie, but setting a longtime-captive killer whale free makes as much sense as introducing a dachshund to the Black Forest. Keiko's saviors could afford to invest thousands of dollars a month in an experiment that didn't work. After all, it was just money and a whale. Both could be replaced. But many of us take the same kind of approach with our lives. We make choices because a decision just feels right. But the road that feels right today may well be the choice we regret tomorrow.

Don't Just Take My Word for It

Read Proverbs 14:12. How can you discern the difference between a path that feels right and one that *is* right? Death in this passage doesn't always mean physical death. What else can die when you choose the wrong path? What decisions have you seen other people make that killed part of their lives and left them to live with the consequences?

Not every choice has life-or-death implications. I doubt if God really cares whether you drink Vanilla Coke or Pepsi Vanilla. But many other decisions you make can have lifelong consequences. How can you tell the difference? Read James 4:13-17. Is saying you want to go into business someday and make a profit wrong in and of itself? Why or why not? What is the key factor in making decisions? How does verse 17 play into this whole process?

Finally (and yeah, I know I have you flipping all over your Bible today), turn to Proverbs 3:5-6. What does God promise to do in this passage? How can this keep you off the path that leads to death?

> 38

Unintended Consequences

When Stephen climbed out of bed one November day, he didn't immediately start making plans to kill his best friend. In fact, the thought never entered his mind. He and Willie had been friends all their lives. Neither would ever harm the other, except maybe to inflict a few scrapes and bruises from some good-natured wrestling around on the ground. But murder? What kind of sick mind thinks of killing a buddy he grew up with? The only thing the two of them planned to kill that day was the beer in Stephen's refrigerator.

Stephen Brasher never planned to kill Willie Lawson. Maybe that's why he told police the shooting was an accident. When the police arrived on the scene, they found Lawson lying on the ground, lifeless, a bullet wound in his head. It didn't take the experts from the local CSI to figure out who pulled the trigger. The gun belonged to Brasher, and all the fingerprints on the grip were his. He even admitted to the shooting. But he claimed it was an accident. He never planned to kill anyone. It just sort of happened.

The jury disagreed. They heard Brasher say in a taped

statement, "There was [sic] only two beers left, so I took one and I told Willie not to take the other one."[1] Apparently an argument broke out between the two men when Brasher found Lawson sipping on the beer he told him to leave in the refrigerator. The argument escalated until one man was shot in the head. Even after the jury sentenced Stephen Brasher to life behind bars in the Texas prison system, he maintained the shooting was an accident. He never intended to kill his lifelong friend, especially over something as insignificant as a can of beer.

When we're little, grownups ask us what we want to be when we grow up. Most of us bounce between dreams of being the next Michael Jordan to walking on the moon to finding a cure for cancer. As children we have big dreams and think life is something we have to plan for. Yet the turning points for most of us come without planning. We make decisions in the blink of an eye—decisions based not on years of hope and hard work, but on raw emotion or our desire at the moment. And the courses of our lives change. The first domino gets knocked over and gravity takes over. In the end, we find ourselves in a place we never thought we would be. It looks like it had to be an accident because we never planned for it to happen.

Life is a collection of consequences, each one building on the other. Sometimes, our best-laid plans carry far less weight than the decisions we make in the blink of an eye. Where our lives end up is determined more by the wisdom to consistently make right choices than by all our years of education. A lifetime of hopes and dreams can all be undone by one moment of stupidity.

It happened to a man named Saul.

Read 1 Samuel 13:5-14. Saul was the first king of Israel. He hadn't been on the job long when he faced a crisis. Israel's constant nemesis, the Philistines, had gathered their army and were about to attack. Saul's troops were vastly outnumbered and outgunned. Or, I should say, outspeared. His soldiers looked across the valley and completely lost their nerve. Many deserted him, and others went over to the enemy's camp. Saul had to do something to keep them together or the battle would be lost before the first shot was fired. So he took matters into his own hands and did what the Law of Moses said only the priest could do. As luck would have it, he'd no sooner finished than the high priest himself showed up.

I'm sure Saul would claim that his actions were really a big misunderstanding. He didn't intend to undermine Samuel's authority or break God's Law. It all just sort of happened. And he paid the price.

After reading Saul's story, do you think his punishment seems harsh, or was it justified? Does God only give us one chance, and if we blow it, have we blown our whole lives? That doesn't seem fair.

Before you shed any tears for Saul, read 2 Samuel 12:7-14. There you will read about the time the second king of Israel did something far worse than Saul did. David slept with another man's wife and then arranged for him to be killed after she found out she was pregnant. But there was one key difference between David and Saul. Can you see it? You will when you read Psalm 51. David wrote this psalm right after God confronted him with his sin. David repented of his sin. Saul made excuses.

Don't Just Take My Word for It

Our lives are impacted by the consequences of the choices we make. Holding on to Christ means trying to do the right things. But sometimes we still make poor or even destructive choices. However, that doesn't mean God is through with us. Read 1 John 1:8-10. Hiding behind lame excuses only makes the hole we dig for ourselves deeper. But honest repentance and a sincere cry for forgiveness give us a fresh start with God. While forgiveness doesn't mean the consequences of our choices are completely wiped away, God's plan for our lives is bigger than the stupid mistakes we make. Remember that the next time you blow it.

> 39

Skara Brae

Skara Brae died one day, but no one noticed for nearly a week. She was the type of person who kept to herself, even from her friends. A handful of people knew her, but no one knew much about her. She never talked about her life or her past. Not even her closest friends in town knew her exact birthday. She had married young, but the marriage didn't last. Papers found over a year after she died revealed that she had two children, a boy and a girl, although she hadn't talked to either one for years. Her daughter got pregnant back in a time when that brought shame on a family. Skara let that rift completely separate the two of them. I don't know if her daughter even knows she died. No one knows what happened to her son or even if he is still alive.

A few stories drift around about her. Someone said she once worked for a judge, but he didn't know when or where. Even her name is a mystery. She wasn't born with it. At some point she chose to call herself Skara Brae, which is a mysterious, ancient settlement on the coast of Scotland. Skara didn't want anyone to know anything about her, and now they never will.

A ladder still leans against Skara's house. The roof needed work, and the outside of the house still needs to be painted. Everyone in town talks about the house and what a landmark it could be. Walking past it, I always imagined it to be a little like Ma Bailey's boardinghouse in *It's a Wonderful Life*. It is so big I just assumed many people lived there. I never knew Skara lived by herself in a house with seventeen rooms. She stayed in only one. If she didn't feel like talking, she wouldn't answer her phone. Skara liked her privacy. She didn't want anyone knowing her business.

That's why it took several days before anyone called the police to report that something wasn't right. Her mail stayed in the mailbox and her phone just rang, but that wasn't totally out of the ordinary. When emergency workers finally did get into her house, it was too late. Skara died days before anyone could get to her to help her. Her death was a lot like her life. She died alone. No one knows exactly when or how she passed away.

When I first heard the story of Skara Brae, I felt the same emotions I feel when I listen to the Beatles sing "Eleanor Rigby." A group of five or six friends gathered in a northwest corner of a cemetery to tell her good-bye. No one really knew what to say. Finally, one white-haired woman leaning against a walker broke the silence. "All I know," she said in her eighty-year-old voice, "is that Skara Brae was always a good friend to me." One or two other people then shared their stories. All were brief because Skara Brae guarded her privacy like some people guard silver or gold. She never talked about herself, but she was always willing to listen to others tell of their problems.

That's why no one knew Skara struggled to pay the heating bill for her seventeen-room house. Late at night in the middle of winter, she would trudge through the snow to her car, start it up, and huddle next to the heater to get warm. Some weeks she ran out of money before she ran out of bills. As a result she would go without groceries. But she never complained. She never told anyone her struggles. But then again, who would she tell? Little old ladies who live alone are easy to overlook.

Don't Just Take My Word for It

James 1:27 says, "Pure and lasting religion in the sight of God our Father means that we must care for orphans and widows in their troubles, and refuse to let the world corrupt us." This verse is a lot like Skara Brae—easy to overlook, easy to pass over without stopping to see the whole story. Yet this verse also reveals the heart of God. He cares about widows and orphans, and He wants us to care for them as well. And just so you know, the word *orphan* doesn't just mean children who have lost both parents. The word literally means "fatherless." I wonder what James would think of the United States today where the number of children growing up without a dad is at an all-time high.

Holding on to God means grabbing hold of His passions and concerns. Read Isaiah 1:10-17 to hear what those may be. What did you find? Why would God care so much about them? Why would He be more concerned about us caring for widows and orphans than offering Him sacrifices or holding festivals in His honor? Write down your thoughts.

Widows and orphans don't often come knocking on our doors for help. They're usually in the shadows—little old ladies in Victorian houses without family and with very few friends. They don't have anyone to call when the toilet backs up or when they hear a strange noise in the middle of the night. Or, they are the nine-year-old kids down the street who always seem to be in trouble, the kids who live in a house where there's a new man in their mother's life every few weeks. Their names sit on the waiting list at Big Brothers Big Sisters, but there always seem to be more names than volunteers.

If James or Isaiah could stand in your room and expand on the verses you just read, what would they tell you to do? A Skara Brae lives in every town. What would God have you do for her?

> 40

Beyond Impossible

For forty days he stayed up on top of the mountain. It was his second trip. And just like his first jaunt up the mountain, Moses didn't eat or drink anything for forty days. He shouldn't have survived. Under normal circumstances, the human body will last only a few days without water. But Moses' circumstances weren't normal. He wasn't alone on top of Mount Sinai. God was there. For forty days Moses lay on his face before the King of heaven and earth, begging for mercy. He didn't have time to think about something as trivial as food or water. The fate of three to four million people hung in the balance. Moses stood alone between them and eternal destruction. So he lay on his face pleading with God to spare their lives and forgive them for building and worshipping a golden cow.

Reading the story of Moses' second forty-day stay on top of Mount Sinai in Deuteronomy 9:7-29, I find myself asking how he did it. How did Moses push his body to go ten times beyond normal human endurance? Forty days without food had been done before, and it has been done since. But forty days without water on top of a mountain in the middle of a desert?

He should have shriveled up like a raisin. And he didn't do this just once. Twice Moses engaged in a full forty-day food-and-water fast in the presence of God with only a few days, perhaps a couple of weeks, in between. How did he do it? It's not like he was in peak physical condition. Thumb back to chapter 7 of Exodus and you will find that Moses was over eighty when he strolled up the mountain. Eighty! Not many people half his age would even want to try climbing Sinai, much less survive without water for over a month on top of it.

The answer to this question doesn't matter only to Moses and people who read his story. The secret of his physical survival on top of the mountain is also the key to your spiritual survival in a world that doesn't exactly roll out the red carpet for people who want to live for Christ. Over the past two weeks we've focused on the theme of trying to hold on to God. We explored ways in which our hold on Jesus is put to the test day after day. There are times when our grip on God seems tenuous at best. We can feel His fingers slipping through ours. We try to hold on, but so many things in our lives try to pry our hands away. And some days we just want to let go. Going against the flow wears us out. The more fatigued we become, the less the payoff seems worth the effort. I have a friend who even went so far as to yell at God, "I don't need this anymore! Leave me alone!"

God didn't answer my friend's prayer. He didn't leave my friend alone for the same reason He didn't let Moses die on top of Mount Sinai. Moses' physical survival during his forty-day fast from all food and water didn't depend on Moses but on God. The Lord Himself kept Moses alive. Jesus said, "Man does not live on bread alone, but on every word that comes from the mouth of God" (Matthew 4:4, NIV). Through his twin forty-day fasts Moses discovered these words to be true. Sitting in the presence of God, he had everything he needed for life. Not only did he survive the experience, but when he walked down from the mountain, Moses' face glowed with the glory of God. He had never been more alive.

While you will never find yourself on top of a fiery mountain standing face-to-face with God, you will find your faith put to the test as you walk through life. Some of the friends you've grown up with, friends who at one time talked about loving God and wanting to serve Him, will take a different path. They'll leave you wondering how firm your grip on Christ really is. Then there are the questions. They'll hit you from every side as you think through all the beliefs your parents and pastors taught you about God when you were a kid. You'll have to sort out what you really believe and why. How will your faith survive?

It will survive because your spiritual survival doesn't depend on how strong you are but on how strong God is. While you struggle to keep hold of His hand, another hand surrounds you. His touch is so soft that you may not even notice it, but His hand is there, holding on to you. God doesn't just grab your hand. He puts you entirely into His hands. This doesn't mean that the journey will ever be simple, nor does it mean that you will never wrestle with doubt. Yet in the midst of the doubts, in the midst of those circumstances that make you want to give up and walk away, the Lord gives you this promise:

> My sheep listen to my voice; I know them, and they
> follow me. I give them eternal life, and they shall never

perish; no one can snatch them out of my hand. My Father, who has given them to me, is greater than all; no one can snatch them out of my Father's hand. I and the Father are one. (John 10:27-30, NIV)

God's hold on your life will never slip.

Don't Just Take My Word for It

Read Psalms 121 and 94:17-22. The psalmist faced physical death if God didn't come through. Most of us are not in danger of our lives being taken, but that doesn't make the trials that threaten to pull us away from the Lord any less severe. When do you find your faith tested the most? Have you ever faced a situation that made you think following Jesus wasn't the best idea? What got you through it? Psalm 121:4 says that God never sleeps but always watches over us. What are some ways you've experienced God watching over you when you needed Him the most?

Not all of our difficult situations are caused by outside forces. Our own desires pull us away from God. Look again at Psalm 121:3. How has God protected you from yourself in the past? Which areas of your life are most in need of God's protection? Read 1 Corinthians 10:13 and 1 John 1:9. God holds on to us by providing a way to escape temptation and by granting us forgiveness when we blow it. Which of these do you need today?

Remember, God promised to hold on to you no matter what. Jesus vowed to never let anyone or anything snatch you out of His hand. You can hold on to Him because He is holding on to you.

Notes

Day 6: Is He Nuts?
1. This story comes out of a visit I made to the prison several years ago. One of the guards told me about the problem of illegals breaking in and finding empty beds.

Day 10: The Red Pill
1. Special thanks to Morpheus (Laurence Fishburne) in *The Matrix* for coining this handy little phrase.

Day 11: From the White House to the Outhouse
1. Paul Johnson, *Modern Times: The World from the Twenties to the Nineties*, rev. ed. (New York: HarperCollins, 1991), p. 456.

Day 16: Bad Guys Finish First
1. Stories of Amin's atrocities can be found in Paul Johnson, *Modern Times: The World from the Twenties to the Nineties*, rev. ed. (New York: HarperCollins, 1991), pp. 533-537.

Day 18: What If They Refuse?
1. C. S. Lewis, *The Problem of Pain* (New York: Macmillan, 1962), p. 128.

Day 20: In Food Pyramids We Trust
1. 2001 Surgeon General's Call to Action to Prevent and Decrease Overweight and Obesity.
2. 2001 Surgeon General's Call to Action to Prevent and Decrease Overweight and Obesity.

Day 21: Man on the Moon
1. William E. Burrows, *This New Ocean: The Story of the First Space Age* (New York: Random House, 1998), p. 431.

Day 22: God Bless This Bomb
1. Gordon Thomas and Max Morgan-Witts, *Enola Gay* (New York: Stein and Day Publishers, 1977), pp. 237-238.
2. Paul Johnson, *Modern Times: The World from the Twenties to the Nineties*, rev. ed. (New York: HarperCollins, 1991), p. 426.

Day 24: Dr. Doolittle's Dream Comes True

1. Institute of Technology and Biosystems engineering, *Understanding Animal Vocalization*, http://www.tb.fal.de/staff/jahns/animal.htm (accessed September 16, 2004).
2. "2002 Best Inventions," *Time*, November 18, 2002, http://www. time.com/time/2002/inventions/tra_bow.html (accessed August 19, 2004). Also see http://bowlingual-translator.com/ (accessed August 19, 2004).

Day 25: Miracle or Statistic?

1. Miles O'Brien, "Spirit landed 'without a hitch,'" *CNN.com*, January 5, 2004, http://www.cnn.com/2004/TECH/space/01/04/otsc.obrien/ (accessed August 19, 2004).
2. NASA Jet Propulsion Laboratory, "Summary," *Mars Exploration Rover Mission*, July 23, 2004, http://marsrovers.jpl.nasa.gov/overview/ (accessed August 19, 2004).
3. *The Canali and the First Martians*, http://aerospacescholars.jsc.nasa.gov/CAS/lessons/L9/4.htm (accessed August 19, 2004).
4. William E. Burrows, *This New Ocean: The Story of the First Space Age* (New York: Random House, 1998), p. 463.

Day 33: Storybook Romance

1. C. S. Lewis, *God in the Dock: Essays on Theology and Ethics* (Grand Rapids, Mich.: Eerdmans, 1970), pp. 108-109.

Day 37: Free Willy

1. "Experts Denounce Call to Kill Keiko," *CNN.com*, September 4, 2002, http://www.cnn.com/2002/WORLD/europe/09/04/norway.keiko/index.html.
2. More details of Keiko's life, free and in captivity, can be found at www.keiko.com.

Day 38: Unintended Consequences

1. Reuters, "Texan killed friend over last beer," December 5, 2002.

About the Author

Mark Tabb is the author of six books, including *Mission to Oz: Reaching Postmoderns Without Losing Your Way* and the 2004 Gold Medallion finalist *Out of the Whirlwind*. His work has appeared in *Discipleship Journal, Rev, Leadership, Christian Parenting Today,* the *Kansas City Star,* and many other publications. Mark is also a contributing editor for Purpose Driven Ministries. In addition to his work as a writer, Mark serves as a volunteer firefighter and chaplain for his local fire department. He and his family live in Indiana. To learn more or to contact Mark, check out his website at www.marktabb.com or e-mail him at mark@marktabb.com.